CONTENTS

SERIES EDITORS' INTRODUCTION

Applied qualitative research broadly entails the design and completion of an ethnographic project in the service of an other-than-academic client. Over this century, qualitative researchers have proven to be especially resourceful in addressing public sector problems. This applied contribution has its origins in the work of cultural anthropologists who assisted colonial administrations and the social work of Chicago School sociologists who studied immigrant populations and social change in the urban environment.

In this 45th volume of Sage's Qualitative Research Methods Series, Marilyn Mitchell reports on another variant of applied qualitative research that meets the demands of the private sector. One subculture of qualitative researchers in the private sector is shown to be composed of practitioners employed by advertising agencies, consulting firms, and other "supplier side" organizations. Another subculture consists of qualitative researchers in the multidisciplinary research departments of large organizations, as well as those who conduct studies based in an assortment of other client side work environments. Qualitative researchers in these two subcultures are challenged in particular to understand and predict consumer behavior, public and political behavior, and organizational behavior.

Mitchell's *Employing Qualitative Methods in the Private Sector* is a strategic volume that concentrates on how qualitative researchers familiar with the structure of academic work can diversify to become productive in a professional setting marked by a language of contracts, deadlines, and deliverables. This book pulls no punches in discussing how the ethnographic method must be attuned to a system in which research originates in the pragmatic logic of requests for proposals (RFPs) and is constrained by the special problems of project and business management. Mitchell's central thesis is that qualitative researchers do indeed have something to sell and are positioned to be competitive in the private sector. To enlarge the qualitative niche, ethnographers will do well to heed Mitchell's translation advice about how to market qualitative expertise.

> —Marc L. Miller
> John Van Maanen
> Peter K. Manning

EMPLOYING QUALITATIVE METHODS IN THE PRIVATE SECTOR

MARILYN L. MITCHELL
Hewitt Associates, Newport Beach, California

1. PRIVATE-SECTOR RESEARCH SETTINGS

Introduction

Every year companies spend thousands of man-hours and millions of dollars struggling to understand, evaluate and predict human behavior, beliefs, values and attitudes—the very heart and soul of applied social science. And every year academic institutions produce thousands of social science graduates, many more than can ever be absorbed into teaching, most of whom will take jobs that make little use of the skills they worked so hard to acquire. I believe that a better coordinated flow of these researchers into the private sector would result in more fulfilling careers for many social scientists, as well as an improvement in the quality of private-sector research practice.

One of the barriers to a better flow of research and researchers is the lack of easily accessible information outlining how and where social scientists can put their skills to use with private sector employers. This information is not usually part of the social science curriculum, and in most academic institutions it exists only on the most informal basis. Social scientists who

1

have made careers in the private sector have usually come to their positions through some odd concatenation of circumstances, personality, and perseverance, typically with little help and sometimes outright resistance, from their universities.

This book is a modest attempt to fill this information gap. It is designed for those who conduct ethnographic research and who have an interest in private-sector employment. It outlines where private-sector employment opportunities exist and what skills are needed to get and succeed in these jobs.

I have been fortunate enough to work in a number of the categories of private sector jobs described in this volume. My first private sector job was at a think tank, the RAND Corporation. This provided my first glimpse of social scientists working outside academic or government settings, and it was an intoxicating one, both in terms of the types of problems addressed (in this case a comparative study of drug education programs at the junior high and high school levels) and in terms of the budget—about $5 million. That experience expanded my thinking about what types of jobs I might consider and led to later positions in market segmentation and prediction (at Nissan North America), in ethnic market research (at Hispanic Market Connections), and human resources consulting (at Hewitt Associates). My career has been both enjoyable and well remunerated, and I am very aware how lucky I was to stumble upon it. It is my hope that this volume will provide at least a partial map for those who are considering a similar path. This book assumes a few things:

1. You already have ethnographic research skills such as interviewing, surveying, applying statistical methods, analyzing data, and writing up results. This is not a book about mastering methods. It is a book about how to get paid for mastery you already have or can easily acquire.

2. You do not have an antipathy for commerce. If you really do not go along with the notion of research findings being bought and sold, you are not going to be happily employed in the private sector and this book is a waste of your time. If you disdain the marketplace, stay out of the bazaar.

3. You can do a meaningful self-assessment about whether or not you have the habits (like turning things in on time and showing up for work every day) and personality traits (such as ambition, salesmanship, and focus) that the private sector values. As a social scientist, you should be able to evaluate both yourself and your potential employer and judge whether you have an acceptable match.

Private-sector research settings can be classified into two major categories, supplier side and client side. The supplier side includes consumer research companies, advertising agencies, consultants, think tanks, and freelance researchers. On the client side are the research departments of companies that provide a wide array of goods and services. Although these two types of settings exhibit considerable methodological overlap, they differ sharply in terms of working environment.

Supplier Side Settings

The private-sector supplier side is by far the largest employer of social science researchers outside academia. There are more than 3,000 consumer research companies, 1,500 ad agencies, 1,000 consulting firms, and dozens of think tanks in the United States. In addition, there are an unknown number of freelance researchers, presumably numbering in the thousands. Although there is considerable variation from firm to firm, a few key characteristics typify supplier side research settings. In general, supplier side work has the following characteristics:

1. It is project-driven—supplier side work comes and goes on a project-by-project basis. Work flow may vary widely based on time of year, economic conditions, product cycles, business cycles, and the financial health of key clients or client industries. For example, a firm that specializes in political opinion polls and focus groups will expect increased business during presidential election years. A firm that tracks advertising awareness will be tied to increases and decreases in advertising expenditures. A consultant specializing in organizational culture studies will be influenced both by general business cycles and trends in human resource management. And a firm that does consumer research in a growth industry, such as over-the-counter drugs, will (at least for a while) face expanding opportunities regardless of economic conditions.

2. It is specialized—although some large research firms describe themselves as "full service," this is at best a relative term. No research company or consultant is proficient in all types of research for all possible clients. Most supplier side firms and individuals are specialized by methodology, market, client industry, or geographic region.

3. It is high-risk, high-reward work—compared to academic, government, or client side jobs, supplier side research offers less in terms of job security. The flow of work is dependent on a number of factors, many of which are outside the control of the researcher. In exchange for this lessened job security, the supplier side offers a number of rewards. Chief among these is the potential for earnings well above those of most researchers in other settings. In addition, advancement can be much more rapid than in other milieus. Suppliers with well developed businesses also have the opportunity

to experience perks common to the business world such as first-class travel, dining, and entertainment. And most rewarding of all, supplier side researchers often have the opportunity to see their research results made real, as client companies use the research findings to transform their organizations, products, and services.

CONSUMER RESEARCH FIRMS

Consumer research firms exist in a wide variety of sizes and specialties. They are prime private sector employers for social scientists, since they are in constant need of both methodological expertise and impress-the-client credentials. With over 3,000 firms in the industry, consumer research opportunities exist for social scientists with almost any imaginable combination of research skills, geographic preference, or personal style. The Greenbook, published each year by the American Marketing Association, is the primary directory of consumer research firms (see References).

The most numerous players in the consumer research industry are small firms providing basic research services on a local level. Often these firms will consist of little more than a focus group facility and a small telephone bank for recruiting research participants. These firms may operate in shopping malls (where they will do mall-intercept recruiting as well as recruiting by phone), in office buildings, or in stand-alone suburban locations.

These firms may or may not have actual research professionals on staff. If they do, they are often the owners of the company, who will hire themselves out as focus group moderators and write up summary reports of focus group proceedings. The credentials of such researchers vary widely; some are PhD level scientists, while others may have no formal social science training at all. In many cases, however, there will be no researchers on staff. In these cases the clients of the focus group facility will provide their own moderator, or the focus group facility operator may recommend a freelance moderator.

Some small firms offer services beyond focus group facilities and recruiting. Most of these fall into the category known as field-and-tab houses. The "field" in field and tab refers to fieldwork (in this usage, fieldwork means solely data collection), most typically in the form of telephone interviewing, although some firms have staff available for face-to-face survey work. The most prominent feature of a field-and-tab operation is its telephone bank. These consist of sophisticated telephone workstations, typically including a monitor that displays the survey instrument and allows the interviewer to record responses directly into a computer file. This file then becomes the basis of the "tab" part of the operation, the creation (either in hard copy or on-line) of a book of cross-tabs of key variables. This data file may also be subjected to whatever statistical manipulations are needed to illuminate the research findings.

Compared to focus group facility firms, field-and-tab houses are relatively sophisticated operations. Field and tab work requires considerable professional expertise in sample design and management, interviewer training and supervision, and data input, auditing and cleaning. It also requires a substantial investment in hardware and software (there are dozens of programs specialized to aid telephone interviewing), both of which must be constantly updated to keep pace with the rapid advancements in interviewing and data processing technology. Whereas some field-and-tab houses are essentially Mom-and-Pop operations, most are considerably larger, and a number are subsidiary operations of regional or national level firms.

A recent addition to the field-and-tab arena has been firms specializing in the administration of surveys through electronic formats. Specialties include machine-readable surveys, surveys done on-line through local area networks (LANs), e-mail, or on Internet sites, and surveys using automated response technology (these include surveys in which the respondents key in their answers rather than speaking to an interviewer). As communications technology proliferates, these specialties will undoubtedly occupy a bigger place in the research spectrum.

Regional market research firms are the next step up in size and methodological sophistication. Often these are local firms that have grown up with a key client, a particular client industry, a specialized methodology or a key consumer market. For example, the Detroit area has a number of sizable research firms that are primarily dependent on clients in the automotive industry. Washington D.C. has several firms that have their roots in election polling and political market research, and Los Angeles boasts some big companies that are primarily dependent on the entertainment industry. Some firms specialize in data collection methods that are linked to their industry specialty and require logistical capabilities beyond those of a focus group operation or a field-and-tab house. Examples of these include vehicle design and marketing clinics (which require huge facilities, specialized transport, and high security); food product testing (which requires highly controlled kitchen facilities and retail test markets); and overnight demographic and acceptance testing for movies (which requires both movie screening facilities and the ability to produce a full printed report in less than twelve hours). More recently, some regional firms have sprung up that specialize in particular consumer markets, especially ethnic markets. These firms are typically located in urban areas with a high concentration of minority residents.

A relatively small number of market research firms can be considered truly national or multinational in scope. These firms usually have offices in several major cities and have links to research companies in other countries (sometimes in the form of joint ventures or wholly owned subsidiaries). An important distinction between national and regional firms is that national firms often get some portion of their revenue from syndicated or multiclient studies. Unlike proprietary projects, syndicated studies are not commissioned by a particular client but rather are done solely by the research firm. The finished report and data are then sold to whoever wishes to buy. Every large client industry has one or more syndicated studies that are bought by most industry participants. The large research firms use these studies, often accompanied by lavish report presentations, to get access to decision makers in client companies. Examples of well known syndicated studies include media ratings done by firms like A. C. Neilsen and I. R. I., the MONITOR study of consumer attitudes conducted by Yankelovich Partners, and the J. D. Power and Associates surveys of automobile quality and customer satisfaction. Some opinion polls are also done on a syndicated basis, although many are sponsored by a single client or client group, such as a media conglomerate.

Multiclient studies are also generally conducted in two major categories—omnibus studies and coalition studies. In an omnibus study, the research firm defines the group of consumers to be surveyed (and sometimes a core group of questions) and each sponsor simply purchases space in the questionnaire (either by item or by interviewer minutes) for proprietary questions. In coalition studies, the research company acts as a broker/coordinator for a group of firms with similar research interests, persuading and helping them to pool their budgets to research a particular topic. In some of these cases, the clients will all share a common final report, whereas in others, each client will get a customized version.

Whereas national firms get some of their revenue and much of their visibility through syndicated work, they get most of their profit from proprietary research. These companies are the ones most likely to do multiregion, national, or multicountry studies. These include multisite qualitative studies, national telephone or direct mail surveys, or product testing and test marketing. The quantitative portions of these studies are usually number crunched at a heavily automated central processing facility that can streamline the handling of large samples. Telephone interviewing for these companies is also usually consolidated at one or several locations. In the United

States, telephone interviewing operations are usually located in the North-Central or Mountain regions, where labor costs are moderate, time zone inconvenience is minimized and potential interviewers do not have pronounced regional accents. Qualitative work, especially that of focus groups, is less likely to be centralized and is often handled at the regional office nearest the client or at the location nearest the qualitative researcher team.

ADVERTISING AGENCIES

Like consumer research firms, ad agencies come in a range of sizes and specialties. There are approximately 1,500 of them in the United States, and the majority of these firms do at least a small amount of research. Ad agencies are more likely than consumer research companies to rely heavily on qualitative research. In part this reflects limited research budgets that cannot usually accommodate the sampling costs of survey research as well as production schedules that dictate very short turnaround times. The use of qualitative methods is also related to industry tradition in which the "creatives" (writers and graphic artists) have status over sales and administrative staff (known as "suits"). Creatives are almost universally allergic to numbers and are suspicious that quantitative research will be used by uninspired suits to snuff out any spark of creativity. But creatives are desirous of seeing their work improved and validated by consumer response and therefore more readily embrace qualitative techniques. Focus groups and small sample copy testing (proposed print ads) or story board testing (scripts for proposed broadcast ads) are among the most commonly used methods in ad agency research.

Whereas all but the smallest consumer research firms have some professional researchers on staff, only the regional or national ad agencies are large enough to support a full-time researcher, group or department. Large agencies may have a central research group that handles work for all their clients, or they may have specific research personnel who are permanent members of the team assigned to a particular client account. In the small to mid-size firms, the research function is almost always centralized and in some cases may consist of a single person.

Whether the research department is large or small, it will probably function in two ways—as a direct supplier of research services and as a broker purchasing services for the agency. If there is at least one person who functions as a researcher, this person or group will probably conduct focus groups or one-on-one interviews for some of the agency's clients. This activity allows the agency to keep the money allocated for research in-house, while still getting some sort of feel for how the market will respond to the agency's output. The personnel performing these services at ad agencies range from complete amateurs to extremely experienced social scientists. Depending on the expertise and ethics of the firm involved, these research efforts range from genuine attempts to evaluate advertising communications to thinly disguised advocacy of the creative effort. If you are considering working for an ad agency as either an employee or a freelancer, you would be wise to learn in advance where the agency stands in this regard.

Only the largest ad agencies have research departments big enough to conduct quantitative research projects in-house. For quantitative work, agencies usually behave as clients rather than suppliers, hiring a market research firm to do the actual study. Usually the person or group assigned to the research function at the agency will interview market research firms, solicit bids for the proposed project, select the winning bidder, and oversee the conduct of the research, delivery, and presentation of the research findings.

CONSULTING FIRMS

Like ad agencies, consulting firms come in a variety of sizes and specialties. Consultants range from one-person freelance operations to huge multinational firms employing thousands of people. Any firm whose consulting specialty includes elements of human behavior will at least occasionally conduct social science research. Just a few of the types of consulting work that offer research opportunities include the following: product design, new product launches, target market identification, work efficiency and safety, ergonomic design of products, crowd behavior, disaster recovery, business turnarounds, business evaluations, opinion polling, communications design and effectiveness, brand image development, change facilitation, human resources strategy, corporate culture, employee opinion and satisfaction, and customer/vendor/product interface design.

Most consulting firms are specialized, focused on providing solutions to a particular category of business problems. In consequence, the size, structure, and composition of consulting firm research departments is quite varied. Consulting firms that conduct research on a regular basis generally hire senior level social scientists (often lured from a university or better yet, from a competing firm), and some have sizable support staffs in the form of data analysts, interviewers, coders, and report processors. The mix of qualitative and quantitative work varies by firm, but most do at least some of each. Due to the confidential nature of most consulting work, these firms tend to do almost all of their research in-house, making minimal use of freelancers and outside research firms.

Unless you are willing to work your way up through the ranks from coder or data processor, you generally need to have a substantial research track record to be hired by a consulting firm. Research consultants who have direct contact with clients must also be rock solid in terms of general business skills; orderly in project management, good at communicating with clients, impressive and effective at meetings, smooth and informative at presentations. Working conditions tend to be fairly demanding—lots of deadlines, long hours (consulting firm personnel practically brag about how many hours per week they put in), lots of travel, and pressure from clients who expect a great deal in terms of both attention and results (and since they are paying $200-$500 per hour for consulting time, why shouldn't they?). Successful research consultants in larger firms can expect six-figure salaries, business perks (premium travel and entertainment, company vehicle or vehicle subsidy, etc.) and the opportunity to work on high-budget, high-visibility research projects.

Each consulting firm has a unique persona and often this persona is a key element in the firm's marketing efforts. Some emphasize rank, hierarchy and credentials (e.g., McKenzie Consulting, which specializes in business strategy and resource allocations studies), others have egalitarian approaches (Hewitt Associates, a leading human resource and organization culture consultant). Some focus more on technology, systems and procedural solutions (Andersen Consulting, which focuses on movement of data and information in organizations), and others offer an array of highly individualistic "stars" (Global Business Network, a leader in multinational predictive studies). If you pursue work with a consulting firm, be sure that you are comfortable with the company's overall style, because a 50-or 60-hour work week can feel pretty long if you are not in sympathy with your colleagues.

THINK TANKS

Think tanks operate in the fuzzy-edged space somewhere between private sector, public sector, and academic social science. Each think tank has its own unique culture and norms, growing out of its particular combination of funding sources, institutional history, and primary research focus. In general, think tanks conduct research that is in some way related to public policy issues, although much of this research is funded by nonpublic sources. At most think tanks, project funding comes from some combination of government grants, charitable or religious foundation grants (from such entities as the Ford Foundation, the Conrad Hilton Foundation, etc.), and political or semipolitical organizations. Research specialties are dictated by the founding mission of the institution and the interests of the funding sponsors—the Brookings Institution focuses primarily on economics, the Heritage Foundation on conservative political issues, the East-West institute on Pacific Rim studies, the RAND Corporation on U. S. public welfare and global strategy.

Almost all think tanks hire social science researchers at both entry and more experienced levels. Because these institutions are intermediate between academia and the business world, they offer researchers an attractive point of transition. Academic credentials are generally well respected in think tanks, and hiring authorities are willing and able to see the relationship between academic work and similar research in more applied settings. The primary issues for those seeking work with a think tank are comfort with the political and research focus of the institution and access (these jobs are not numerous; some think tanks are effectively private clubs). Working environments at think tanks are more like academic settings than like businesses, and salaries for most think tank positions are intermediate between the two. If you are interested in influencing public policy or like the bully pulpit of newspapers covering your findings and can find a think tank whose goals are in concert with your own, these entities offer research opportunities that are well funded, highly visible, and socially important.

FREELANCING

Freelance researchers can operate in two ways: They may contract directly with client side firms, or they may contract to supplier side firms, in effect becoming the suppliers to the suppliers. Freelance operators generally mirror the characteristics of the research industry as a whole, with most freelancers having a specialty in a particular methodology, consumer market, or industry. The most common categories of freelancers are focus group moderators and interviewers, statisticians, and report writers.

For qualitatively trained social scientists, freelance work as a focus group moderator or expert interviewer is often one of the easiest points of entry into the private sector. Some clients do not distinguish between work done in academic and commercial settings (indeed, for many clients the whole area of social science research is pretty murky), and some even have the notion that work done by someone whose experience is mostly academic will produce findings that are more scientific or objective. Small clients, especially those with small budgets, often do not have regular relationships with market research firms and may make a good starting point for a beginning freelancer. You can reach such clients by developing a relationship with a focus group facility or other small market research firm or by approaching potential clients directly through your own marketing activities.

Freelancing is especially appropriate and lucrative for social scientists with exotic methodological capabilities. For example, if you have developed a familiarity with a hard-to-reach group that some marketer is interested in (these range from members of ethnic/linguistic minorities to social elites) you can sell your specialized ability to communicate with and explain the behavior of these groups. The more unusual and commercially important the group, the more valuable the access.

Many academic social scientists freelance on a part-time basis, supplementing both their incomes and their research interests. It is also possible to freelance full-time, especially once you have established a base of clients sufficient to provide an adequate flow of work. Freelancing is a good choice for those who like a great deal of autonomy, who are able and willing to do 100% of their own marketing, who have the self-discipline to manage a business in an unstructured environment, and who will not get an ulcer wondering when (and if) the next paycheck will arrive. For most practitioners, the freelance work environment is characterized by big swings in work flow, alternating between not-enough-to-live and way-too-much-to-do. It can also be somewhat isolated and is not a good choice for someone who enjoys daily interaction with work colleagues or prefers teamwork. But for those who can handle the challenges, freelancing offers a great deal of freedom (for example, the clothing-optional dress code for report writing and making client phone calls—you will not get that at most jobs) and maximum opportunity to balance earnings, time off, and research interests in a way that is uniquely your own.

Client Side Settings

Many social scientists in private sector practice are employed directly by corporations. Almost any company that produces goods or services for consumers on a national basis or has a large (5,000+) employee base will have at least a few researchers in-house. Compared to supplier side settings, client side work has the following characteristics:

1. It is rhythmic—most client side research settings have a predictable flow of work, with many projects done on a repeated basis, either of product life cycles or annually or semiannually. Because work is usually organized on a project basis, researchers can usually predict their busy or slow times weeks or months in advance. Along with this predictability comes some

degree of sameness. Tracking studies that are done on a repeated basis every quarter, year or whatever, offers little opportunity for innovation in design or methodology. Fortunately, most client side jobs intersperse tracking studies with stand-alone work that has more room for creative social science.

2. It is methodologically generalized and topic specialized—few client settings are large enough to support researchers with a narrow methodological focus. In general, client side social scientists will be involved in studies that embrace a variety of techniques, both qualitative and quantitative. Client side settings are specialized, however, in that all studies will somehow relate to the client's specific product, service, or department. When considering a client side position, do not underestimate the degree to which this will influence the day-to-day work environment. You do not have to be in love with the product in order to do good research, but it sure helps. If you just cannot get excited about cars, cosmetics, or breakfast cereal, you should think long and hard before accepting a position in a company that lives and dies for its product. Similarly, if you feel that human resources is the department where brains go to die, you may not be cut out for that job researching organizational effectiveness at Megabucks Corporation.

3. It is corporate—the difference between doing research as a supplier and doing research as an employee can be dramatic (even with the same company). As an employee you will be exposed to company politics, hierarchies, norms, and traditions. Once hired, you will not get to choose your boss or your assignments, although you may have a great deal of autonomy about how to get the assignments done. In general, advancement in client side positions is slow and steady, with some degree of visible career path. Researchers are not usually in line for CEO, and in many companies their careers top out at the director or vice-presidential level. If you have a strong desire to run the whole show, you should consider a client side job only if it is a sensible stepping-stone to your ultimate career goal.

CORPORATE RESEARCH DEPARTMENTS

Almost all large companies that provide either goods or services to consumers will have a research department. Some have more than one, often having one group of researchers devoted to product and service development, while another group helps support marketing activities (for you academic types, marketing = sales + advertising + promotions + public relations—see Kotler's *Marketing Management*). These research departments function in much the same way as those in advertising agencies, performing some research and analytical activities themselves but also acting as brokers in selecting and hiring outside market research firms. Examples of industries

13

in which social scientists are hired in-house include the following: food manufacturing, food service, packaged goods, broadcasting, telecommunications, consumer electronics, computers, automotive, financial services, real estate development, pharmaceuticals, office equipment, transportation, and every category of retailing.

There are some key differences between corporate research jobs and similar on-staff positions in advertising agencies. Companies that take consumer opinion seriously are likely to have research departments that are both large and well staffed. Big consumer products firms typically will have at least a few PhD level social scientists, whereas such backgrounds are quite rare at ad agencies. Research budgets can be substantial; some range into the tens of millions of dollars on an annual basis. And the role of the researcher usually is divorced from advocacy for a particular product or marketing approach. Whereas no corporate environment is completely free of the pressures of company politics, research departments generally get some space in which to act as objective reporters of consumer sentiment.

Naturally, the research work environment in a corporation will mirror its overall white collar milieu. Positions are typically salaried, with a fairly well defined career ladder. Depending on the overall role and prestige accorded to research at a particular firm, social scientists may be found well up among the ranks of middle management and occasionally (especially in consumer package goods firms) may reach executive rank.

HUMAN RESOURCES DEPARTMENTS

Whereas human resources departments are most likely to purchase research services from suppliers, a few of the very largest companies (those with more than 5,000 employees) actually have their own in-house researchers. These researchers function in ways similar to those in advertising agencies, both acting as brokers for services purchased from suppliers and as principal researchers for projects conducted entirely in-house.

It is fairly unusual for even a very large company (one with 100,000 or more employees) to have a full-time dedicated research position within the human resources function. Typically, scientists in these positions will combine their research duties with some other aspect of the human resources function, such as compensation management, program design and administration, performance management, staffing and recruiting, training, and organizational effectiveness. Social scientists with a specialty in these areas may enjoy a high-variety work life that includes both the intellectual rigors of social science and hands-on management. There is great satisfaction in taking a project all the way from business problem through research to implementation of the results.

Social scientists considering work in this interesting area should make a careful decision about whether they seriously wish to work from inside rather than from outside a corporate human resources department. Some companies place great emphasis on the human resources function, including it in strategic planning at the highest levels and giving great emphasis to data collection and analysis. In other firms, human resources is not much more than the policy police, with constrained budgets and limited career paths. This can also be a highly political department and researchers may be under tremendous pressure to come up with the "right" answers (those that agree with the opinion of some vocal executive). Some scientists may prefer to work in this field as consultants, rather than expose themselves to the full brunt of company politics.

2. RENAMING YOUR SKILLS

This chapter provides a brief description of qualitative and quantitative social science research methods as they are used in the private sector. Assuming that you are already familiar with a wide array of methods and that you are competent in them, the emphasis is on information that will enable you to make the translation to commercial research. Thus, this is more a description of categories and settings than a detailed how-to course.

Even though I have followed the traditional division into qualitative and quantitative, many private sector projects will partake of both. It is common to use qualitative techniques such as depth interviews or focus groups to provide the preliminary description of a domain, then to follow with a quantitative description that relies on a survey. Alternatively, qualitative techniques may be used following a survey or mapping exercise in order to probe the reasons behind the numerical findings. Much of the fun of commercial research comes from picking and choosing an array of methods that most fully and effectively illuminates the problem at hand.

Qualitative Research

Qualitative research, most typically in the form of depth interviews or focus groups, is a staple of the private-sector research world. In many ways, markets, business organizations, and political movements of interest to the private sector are subcultures with their own sets of relevant categories, specialized vocabularies, and characteristic behaviors. Interviewing active participants in one of these groups is analogous to interviewing knowledgeable informants during anthropological fieldwork. And just as good ethnography enables us to understand a culture in its own terms, a properly conducted interview-based description enables the reader to understand a particular group in its commercial, organizational, or political context.

An important similarity between ethnographic interviewing and interview-based descriptions is the crucial role of the interviewee selection process (Johnson, 1990). The anthropological literature is rife with examples of ethnographic success or failure based on fortuitous or ill-fated selection of informants. The same combination of representativeness, knowledgeability, and access that characterizes good cultural informants must be sought in potential interviewees for private sector group descriptions.

The norm in anthropological fieldwork is to rely heavily on one-on-one interviews with a limited number of key informants. In most cases group interviews are either nonexistent or occur on only the most casual and incidental basis. It is also common in fieldwork to choose at least some informants who occupy unusual or important social roles or who have specialized cultural knowledge. In contrast, the private sector emphasis is usually on interviewing representative participants; "experts" are generally screened out during the interviewee selection process. One-on-one interviews are not rare, but the majority of interviews are conducted with groups of varying sizes. The three key private sector interviewing paradigms are depth interviews, focus groups, and ethnographic interviewing.

DEPTH INTERVIEWS

Depth interviews are done on either an individual or very small group basis. Common terminology for individual interviews is "one-on-ones," for twosomes "dyads" or "pairs" and for threesomes "triads." It is typical to do this type of interview for topics that are not conducive to group interaction, for example, topics that may cause interviewees to make embarrassing revelations about themselves or where it is important that respondent opinions not be influenced by the reactions of others (Andreasen, 1988). This interviewing method is also appropriate when the interview plan includes some sort of activity such as a pile sort or laddering exercise that is best done on an individual basis. A laddering exercise is a structured interview in which the underlying decision process or structure is revealed by successive layers of questioning. It is closely akin to the ethnographic interviewing paradigm detailed by Spradley (Spradley, 1979). For example, if a respondent says he prefers Jeeps because they are tougher, the interviewer responds with a question such as "What makes them tougher?" When the respondent replies, "Well, they are built better, of stronger materials," the researcher might say, "What kind of materials?" This goes on until the respondent stops introducing new terms (or until he throttles the interviewer). Watching this technique in action is akin to observing a 5-year-old endlessly pestering a parent with "Why?" questions.

Individual or small group interviews may also be chosen simply because of the difficulty of scheduling larger groups with certain categories of respondents; for example, if you need to interview Spanish-speaking physicians who treat cardiac patients, it may be impossible to get more than two or three together at one time. And in organizational studies, it is common to do individual interviews with executives due to the combination of tight schedules, high status, and need for confidentiality.

Depth interviews are usually exploratory in nature and are used when the client or researcher needs to refine and expand her understanding of a topic or group. In cases where the small group size was chosen for reasons of convenience, depth interviews may be of a more focused nature, with interviewees doing laddering, categorizing, sorting, ranking or rating tasks. Exploratory interviews are usually fairly long, ranging from 30 minutes to one hour. The more tactical interviews are typically shorter and range from about 15 to 30 minutes. The shorter form is especially favored in advertising research, in which individuals or small groups are shown one or more ads, storyboards, slogans or concept statements and then are quickly interviewed to ascertain their responses.

Although depth interviews are very useful, they are relatively expensive. Sample sizes are usually limited (less than 30) and often driven by budget or time constraints. The amount of interviewer time and rental of appropriate facilities raises the cost per participant well above most other varieties of commercial research. Many projects that can benefit from research simply do not warrant the sort of expenditures that are required for depth interviews. This has served to limit the use of this method and been one of the forces behind the popularity of focus groups as a qualitative research method.

FOCUS GROUPS

The mainstay of private sector qualitative research is the focus group. An estimated 150,000 focus groups are conducted each year in the United States alone, representing more than $500 million in revenue. To some private sector clients, research and focus groups are synonymous, and they rarely utilize any other method. Others use a variety of methods but seldom conduct a major project that does not include focus groups as one of its components. If you plan to make any substantial proportion of your private sector income from qualitative research, focus groups must be an integral part of your repetoire.

Focus groups are interviews with eight to twelve participants. Some researchers also conduct minifocus groups of four to six participants. A typical group lasts one and a half to two hours. Although focus groups can be conducted in any location that will accommodate the participants in reasonable comfort and privacy, most (especially in consumer and political research) are done at dedicated facilities. Focus group facilities can be found in all major cities and many smaller ones (most are listed in the American Marketing Association Greenbook). A typical facility has one or more meeting rooms, each furnished with a conference table that can seat an entire group. Some tables are custom designed to allow the researcher, referred to as the moderator or facilitator, an unobstructed line of sight to all members of the group. Rooms are almost always equipped with microphones for recording group proceedings, and better facilities will dual-record to prevent loss of data due to equipment failure. Most rooms also have a two-way mirror on one wall, with an observation room on the other side of the mirror. Clients or fellow researchers can sit in the observation room and watch the groups without disturbing the flow of the interview. In some cases the room is also equipped with a video camera (some are fixed position, others can be remote aimed from the observation room) which will allow for visual recording of the group. It is also common to videotape from the observation room (this usually requires a live camera operator) by shooting through the two-way mirror.

Most recruiting of focus group participants is done by staff at the focus group facility, using a screening questionnaire and sampling profile provided by the researcher or client. The facility takes responsibility for contacting and screening potential participants, issuing the invitations and location directions to them, and signing them in (and sometimes rescreening) when they arrive. Most facilities charge for recruitment on a per-head basis. Participants are normally paid for their time. The amount of payment will vary depending on the rarity of potential participants that match the screening profile, their social and income class, and the nature of the interview topic. Participants who are easy to recruit may receive payments of only $20-$30 for a two-hour group, while affluent consumers being interviewed about luxury products may get over $100. And members of high-salary professions, such as doctors or lawyers, may need an inducement of several hundred dollars to appear at a group. In some cases the participants may be offered gift certificates or donations to charity in their names in lieu of cash. These choices are popular with affluent participants who might resist the notion that they would sell their time for only $75 or $100 dollars but might love to get a nice restaurant meal or pick a charity to receive the same amount.

Focus groups done in corporate settings, such as those conducted to collect employee opinions, are less likely to be conducted in a focus group facility. In many cases, a conference room at the client's site will serve this purpose. This will limit the potential for client sponsors to observe the groups, especially if the focus group topic is a sensitive one. In these settings, researchers should be very careful to preserve the confidentiality of participants and to protect them against retaliation from their sponsors.

Recruitment in corporate settings will probably be done by taking a random sample from the payroll or other similar list of employees. If this task is handled by someone within the client firm, care should be taken to ensure that the focus group does not dengenerate into a sample of convenience. Typically, employees do not receive extra pay for attending a focus group, since they are usually being paid for their time anyway. When practical, it is nice to offer them some noncash incentive for participating, such as a T-shirt or hat with the client's logo.

It is customary to provide some sort of refreshment to participants, such as soft drinks and snacks or sandwiches if the group is held near a mealtime. As with cash payments, the type and elaborateness of the food should be appropriate to the group and topic. Clients who are observing the groups must also be provided with an array of food and drinks, normally including a hot meal if there is more than one group in a row or if the groups occur in the evening. Most focus group facilities have arrangements with nearby restaurants and can help with food planning. Be certain to find out if your client expects alcohol; many facilities do not routinely provide it. Be aware that giving alcohol to client observers can have unintended results. Use your judgement, especially if the number of client observers is more than one or two people—big gangs of observers are more likely to get rowdy.

Even though most academic social scientists are familiar with interviewing techniques, many have never seen a focus group or been inside a focus group facility. Successful focus group moderation is not identical to one-on-one interviewing and is a highly professionalized specialty. Several research organizations offer training courses that lead to certification as a focus group moderator, and these courses can be worthwhile for people with little exposure to the method. It is also possible to learn through observing groups or videotapes of groups conducted by experienced moderators. In addition, there are several reference books devoted to this technique that the novice moderator can consult (see References and Additional Resources). If you live in an urban area, there are probably one or more focus group facilities nearby. Visiting during slow hours (generally daytimes are slower than nights) is an easy way to become more familiar with the focus group environment. Just tell the manager you wish to see the facility in order to assess its suitability for your future research activities.

Key elements in focus group research are the interaction between group members and the broader coverage of issues that is often stimulated by their exchanges with one another. Since most social science training focuses on one-on-one interviewing, many researchers will have to develop, extend and improve their skills in the areas of group dynamics (a little practice in crowd control comes in handy, too). Training courses, reference books, and viewing focus groups are invaluable in this regard. The other aspect of focus group moderation that catches novices unprepared is the amount of energy that each group requires. When you first move into this arena, make sure that you do not schedule too many groups too close together. You will need time between groups to organize your thoughts and your notes. Also remember that clients, observers, and participants can eat during the focus groups, but the moderator cannot. If you schedule three two-hour groups back-to-back, you will probably be disorganized, exhausted, and hungry by the third group and will not be doing your best.

ETHNOGRAPHIC INTERVIEWING

Because of its intense and comprehensive nature, ethnographic interviewing is relatively rare in private-sector research. Ethnographic interviews differ from one-on-one depth interviews in that they attempt to understand the subject group, product, or activity in its cultural or symbolic context. They are generally less scripted, using more open-ended questions and being more open to following up new information and unanticipated directions. They are also generally much longer and may even be spread over several contacts with each informant. The costs associated with this technique are higher, but ethnographic interviewing can be appropriate for some clients and settings, and these cases offer excellent opportunities for experienced researchers making the transition from academic to commercial research.

The key to private sector use of ethnographic interviewing is the proper selection of clients and research problems. In consumer market research, good clients for ethnographic projects are those who design, make or sell products that involve complex purchase decision processes, high substitutability, and lots of symbolic content. A good example is special occasion food products, such as cookies. Deciding which cookies to buy is quite complicated; there are many products to choose between, there are numerous possible substitutes both within and outside the cookie category, and the use of the product is loaded with symbolic issues: Can you eat them direct from the package or do they belong on a plate? What sorts of occasions can they be served at? Are they for family members or for guests? For adults or for children? Do people help themselves or will they be served? Do they go with certain other foods, beverages, occasions?

Complex group interactions, such as business meetings, can also be prime candidates for ethnographic interviewing. Much of the communication in these meetings is nonverbal, and there can be a great deal of symbolic content in both verbal and nonverbal interactions.

For these categories of products and groups, ethnographic interviewing, especially at the location or occasion of product purchase or use or at key social moments, can be very revealing. People are much better at describing their thoughts and feelings as they happen than after the fact in the unfamiliar setting of a focus group facility. And ethnographic interviewing gives clients the chance to understand behavior in context, including all its rituals (ever see how people eat Oreos?), symbolic depth (ever see anybody buy perfume?), and social complexity (ever see people defer to the opinions of higher ranking people at a meeting?). Field notes from these interviews may include verbatim statements made by the respondent, observer notes about body language and behavior sequences (e.g., someone placed in the driver's seat of a new car will probably touch all the controls and pretend to drive. Those who really like the car may interrupt their pretend driving to primp in the review mirror, obviously imagining themselves being viewed by others in this oh-so-cool vehicle). If the research setting allows it, audio tapes, still photos or videotapes can also be useful.

The biggest barrier to conducting ethnographic private sector studies is the lack of client familiarity with the technique. Clients almost never put out a request for proposals specifying their intention to conduct ethnographic research. If you would like to use this technique, and believe that a particular client will benefit, you will have to sell them on the idea with a research proposal using ethnographic interviewing (see Appendix D). But the results, both for the researcher and the client, can be very satisfying. These studies are enjoyable to design and conduct: Most research subjects are flattered to be chosen for study; the insights gained can be substantial;

and the client can pat himself on the back for having used such an effective and innovative approach.

DIRECT OBSERVATION AND MEASUREMENT OF INTERMEDIATE VARIABLES

Social scientists, especially anthropologists, are used to learning about and analyzing human behavior through straightforward observation and through measurement of intermediate variables that are linked to the variable of interest (Webb, 1981). These important and cost-effective techniques are amazingly underutilized in the private sector. In many cases, clients ignore them because they are unaware of them or do not believe they will yield valuable insights.

As with ethnographic interviewing, the key to using these techniques is proper selection of clients and research problems. These techniques are especially handy when precise quantification is desirable, there is strong reason to believe that participants or respondents cannot or will not accurately report their behavior, and when it is possible to observe the behavior directly or a good intervening variable can be recognized.

A good example of directly observable (but difficult to self-report) behavior is the frequency of lipstick reapplications by women in various settings or over the course of a day. Such behavior is of great interest to cosmetics manufacturers and can be directly observed either by unobtrusive live observers or hidden cameras (if kept within ethical bounds, i.e., placed where people would expect to be observed or where specific permission has been granted). Similar work has been done in assessing the use of automobile stereo controls by drivers and in a variety of other high-frequency or low-salience product use situations. And, of course, considerable research has tracked the movements and activities of people in work settings, with results that often suprise and sometimes embarrass the participants.

Measurements of intermediate variables can be quite innovative. For example, the popularity of museum exhibits has been indirectly measured by noting the wear patterns on the floors or carpets in front of displays, and by measuring the accumulation of smudges on the protective glass (measuring the height of the smudges also allows for an estimate of the age range of viewers). Such measurements have the advantage of low cost for data collection (someone has to clean the glass, anyway), unobtrusiveness, complete privacy for participants, and the opportunity for frequent or continuous measurement over time.

Quantitative Research

In many cases, clients will need more precise measurements than qualitative research can provide. This is particularly true when the client already
has a fairly accurate description of the topic or subject group of interest
and needs to move from discussions of "What are they like?" to such questions as "How many?" "How much?" and "How often?" Broadly speaking,
two major categories of quantitative techniques are used in the private sector: surveys, and mapping and modeling.

SURVEYS

Surveys are the mainstay of quantitative data collection in the private
sector (Bradley, 1982; Luck, 1987; McQuarrie, 1996.) This technique has
a number of virtues. It is familiar to both client and subjects. Within the
accuracy limits of self-reporting, it can be used to collect data on a wide
range of behaviors, attitudes, beliefs and intentions. Surveys may be ad-
ministered via face-to-face interviews (allowing data collection from low-
literacy subjects), by telephone using either live interviewers or automated
response systems, via paper and pencil, or in such electronic forums as
Internet sites, local area networks (LANs), or stand-alone kiosks. And most
important of all, at least from a private sector perspective, surveys yield
numbers, in the form of frequencies and percentages.

Many private-sector audiences, especially those with engineering or
other technical backgrounds, are unable to get comfortable with any research finding that is not backed by numbers. It is the researcher's job both
to generate these numbers and to make sure that the numbers are not bogus
(Kirk & Miller, 1986). To do this, the researcher must thoroughly understand the problem, accurately identify the subject population, do a first-rate
job of sample design and subject selection, construct a valid research instrument, and adhere to professional standards at all stages of questionnaire
administration, data processing, and analysis.

Although survey research is very cost effective on a per subject basis,
the complex sampling schemes and large numbers of interviews required
to produce statistically useful data mean that most surveys are quite costly.
A low-end survey might be as little as $20,000, whereas a major global
effort might reach $1 million. Normally clients only undertake these proj-
ects to illuminate decisions in which they have a lot at stake. A failure at
any step in the research process can produce results so misleading as to
cost your client huge sums of money (faulty survey research played a key
role in the unsuccessful development and launch of New Coke and the

infamous Ford Edsel) and could destroy your reputation. Researchers without survey experience will want to spend substantial time with the vast literature in this area before taking on a survey project for a client.

MAPPING AND MODELING

Most social scientists have some familiarity with techniques used to create maps and models of social phenomena. These techniques range from simple mapping methods such as pile sorts, semantic differentials and rank ordering to complex statistical manipulations such as various forms of regression analysis, principal components analysis, and conjoint analysis. Many quantitative methods that first appear in academic journals will find their way, after a few years, into private-sector research. For example, conjoint analysis had been a standard technique in the academic literature for about 10 years before it found use in modeling the effects of changes in product characteristics on future sales. Quantitatively sophisticated social scientists have their own methodological favorites, and it is likely that yours have found at least occasional application in the private sector. From the perspective of your potential clients, these varied and numerous methods can be broadly clustered into two categories, mapping and modeling.

Mapping is a general term for using quantitative techniques to build pictures or descriptions of a given domain. In the private sector, these might be descriptions of a market, for example, using factor analysis or hierarchical clustering or both as the basis of a market segmentation. Another would be the use of social-network analysis to form the basis of a description of behavior within an organization or to study opinion formation (Iacobucci, 1996). Regardless of the technique used, what mapping methods have in common is that they yield a description that could not be as easily or as accurately elicited from subjects merely by interviewing or observing them. When used appropriately, these techniques also have the virtues of robustness and stability, producing descriptions that can be replicated across different samples within a population, and which do not change capriciously.

Modeling takes description a step further and enables the researcher to make predictions. These may be predictions of changes in market size, market response to a product introduction, expected outcomes of marketing activities, projected voting behavior, or movements in attitudes and beliefs. From the perspective of commercial research, if you have identified independent and dependent variables and postulated a relationship between them, you have moved into the realm of modeling. Commonly used modeling methods include various forms of regression analysis, factor analysis, and conjoint analysis (Kress & Snyder,1994).

As you might expect, the commercial value of well designed models can be huge. An employer who wished to influence employee morale by redesigning employee benefits faces a wide array of design choices within a more-or-less fixed budget. Research that accurately estimates employee response to different benefits designs can pay for itself 100 times over. For a car company, the difference between a successful product launch and a failure can be tens of billions of dollars. With such enormous amounts at stake, modeling projects can be some of the most interesting and lucrative in the private sector.

3. BUSINESS ACTIVITIES THAT REQUIRE RESEARCH

No activity is more crucial to success in the private sector than renaming your skills into the language of business. You can look through the classified ads for the next 10 years without seeing a single search request for a social scientist. But this does not mean that businesses do not need your skills, just that they have other names for them. To become employable in the private sector, you must incorporate business names and business language into your self-description. Fortunately, this linguistic task can be approached using traditional social science methods, in effect doing a mini-ethnography that will enable you to understand and communicate with the business culture you intend to join.

Each industry and consumer research specialty has some customs and vocabulary that distinguish insiders from outsiders. If potential clients and employers are to feel comfortable with you, you need to take on at least enough of this native coloring to make them confident that you understand their business environment. This chapter cannot provide detailed descriptions of the traditions and jargon of all the industries that employ social scientists, but it does provide an overview of the way the private sector thinks and talks about social science research.

To become fluent in the language of the private sector you must recast your frame of reference. Both academic social science and private-sector research concern themselves with the behaviors, beliefs, attitudes and values of groups of people. But private-sector research views them specifically through their relation to key economic and public activities. Thus, an academic anthropologist might view the kinship network of a group in light of its comparison to other kinship arrangements or in relation to other social systems at work in the same group. In the private sector the same anthropologist would view the kinship network in terms of its relationship to consumer behavior, voting patterns, or employee/employer interactions. To rename your skills, you must constantly keep in mind the types of things that business people care about (or at least the ones that they care about enough to budget research dollars for). And you must use terms to describe your skills that will be familiar and recognizable to your private-sector colleagues.

The world of private-sector research on human behavior is divided into three major categories: consumer behavior, public and political behavior, and organizational behavior. All these areas make use of both qualitative and quantitative methods, and each has its own important subcategories, specialties, and outlook. Research-relevant descriptions of each of these key pieces of the commercial research world now follow.

Consumer Behavior

The overwhelming commercial interest in consumer behavior creates the large number of research jobs in market research and advertising. In budget terms, consumer behavior research dwarfs all other categories combined. And no wonder, since understanding and predicting what people will buy guides an enormous amount of commercial activity in such areas as product design, manufacturing, distribution, retailing, and advertising. One way to get a researcher's-eye view of this vast category is to divide it, like Gaul, into three major subcategories: markets, marketing, and sales modeling and predicting.

MARKETS

When the private sector considers consumers in groups, it refers to these groups as markets. Markets may be defined in terms of geography (e.g., the U.S. market, the metropolitan Chicago market), ethnicity/language (the Hispanic market), age (the youth market, the senior market), income (the affluent market), household composition (the families with young children market), propensity to purchase a certain category of product (the new car buyers market) or a mind-set that affects purchases across multiple categories of products (the technophile market, the bargain-hunters market). Although it is pretty easy to come up with words to describe markets of current or potential commercial interest, it is not so simple to make these descriptions precise enough and meaningful enough to support business decisions.

26

It is in adding this degree of precision and meaning to the commercial descriptions of markets that some of the most interesting private-sector social science occurs. In business jargon, improving the descriptions of markets includes two major tasks: segmenting and targeting.

Segmenting

Commercial firms spend substantial research dollars trying to identify and understand potential consumers of products and services. In most categories of consumer goods, customer markets are highly fragmented; for example, there are more than 300 models of automobiles sold in the United States, thousands of brands of shampoo, dozens of styles of telephones. In most categories the products or services offered differ from one another along some set of dimensions; for example, cars differ along such key dimensions as body style, physical size, power and performance, country of origin, price, and brand image. The overall character of a product or service is essentially the sum of its positions along the category-relevant dimensions. But clearly, there are not consumers for all the possible choices of product and service character. It is difficult to imagine any consumer who would be interested in a vehicle with sports car body styling, limited power, a high price, and Eastern European origin. To be commercially successful, producers of goods and services must identify a group of potential buyers that actually exists and understand the product characteristics that these buyers will find most appealing. In commercial research terms, these activities are generally referred to as market segmentation.

The techniques of market description and segmentation are akin to those used in academic settings to describe and identify human collectivities such as communities, cultures, tribes, villages, ethnicities, castes, affiliative associations and classes. The difference is that in the commercial setting the collectivities are identified and described by their responses to a particular category of product and to the possible product positionings along relevant dimensions. These locally defined collectivities may or may not correlate with more broadly defined communities or groups. For example, the group of "potential peanut butter consumers" will cut across ethnic, social class, language, and geographic lines. In contrast, "U. S. consumers of Spanish language television programming" will have a strong correlation with ethnicity.

The larger divisions of consumer collectivities are generally referred to as markets (e.g., new car buyers), while identifiable subgroups within a market are referred to as market segments (e.g., sports car buyers, technophile car buyers). Qualitative and quantitative techniques familiar to most social scientists are the basis of most market segmentations (Berrigan & Finkbeiner, 1992).

Targeting

Targeting is the fraternal twin of market segmentation. Segmentation research describes and to at least some extent quantifies the market potential of market segments. Targeting focuses on selecting and pursuing segments from among those that have been described. Most segmentation projects have some element of targeting either expressed or implied. In some cases, the party who conducts the segmentation research will be expected to recommend specific segments that represent the targets of greatest opportunity for the client. In other cases, the client will simply take the results of the segmentation research and do its target selection as a purely in-house activity. But in case you are asked to participate in target selection, it is vital that you be aware of the key distinctions that distinguish targeting from segmentation.

It is not the case that companies simply determine which market segment represents the most sales (or the most profitable ones) and then go after it. Most companies are limited in their choice of targets by their own histories and situations. A company may be limited in its manufacturing capacity, design capability, or have an existing image that impedes appeal to a particular market segment. A powerful competitor may have an unassailable position within a segment. Or the client company may have a larger strategy that requires targeting a particular segment in order to win or consolidate a broader market position. Because of these factors, effective targeting not only considers the characteristics of the market segments but also those of the client.

From a supplier side standpoint, targeting assignments require three stages of research: identifying and evaluating the market segments, evaluating the client's capabilities and strategies, and making a reasonable alignment between the two. Some client characteristics can be evaluated and matched to targets by MBA-type business analysis: balance sheets, pro forma financial statements, sales forecasts, and the like. But a truly insightful selection of targets requires a broader perspective and one that partakes of the heart and soul of ethnographic understanding. Successful selection of target markets is building a connection between two cultures—the culture of the market segment and the culture of the client company. The ability to identify and communicate these connections is a core competency of good ethnographers and one that can greatly enhance the more mundane types of business analysis that are often employed in target selection. For example, the results of an automotive segmentation study of sedan buyers may identify several groups that, on a purely economic basis, represent attractive potential targets. To make it simple, let's assume there are three, in rank order by market size: a price- and value-oriented group, a safety-oriented group, and a sporty- and performance-oriented group. If you are working with Volvo, you are probably not going to recommend targeting the first group, despite its larger size. It would be unlikely that Volvo could successfully produce a car for this group, as both its internal culture and market image would have to change dramatically.

Even though the example above is trivially easy, others can be much more subtle. You will probably not have an opportunity to do a formal ethnography of your client firm, but ethnographic experience should help you in identifying dimensions along which the client culture and potential target market culture may be profitably aligned.

To do an effective job of targeting, you must blend your ethnographic sense with traditional business analysis, either by adding the business analysis skills to your own capabilities or by working with others trained in such work. The synergies between these skill sets are huge, and the value that the combination brings to clients can be substantial. Do not be afraid to sell this aspect of your ethnographic background and do not hesitate to talk about the cultural aspects of targeting. This is one of the most powerful and salable elements of the ethnographic perspective.

MARKETING

Once a manufacturer or retailer has identified a target market, it will then proceed to spend vast sums of money attempting to actually connect these target consumers to its products or services. Collectively, these activities are referred to as marketing and can be conveniently divided into three major categories: advertising and media consumption, promotions, and public relations.

Advertising and Media Consumption

Advertising is the most ubiquitous (some would say iniquitous) marketing activity. Advertising revenue is the primary support of broadcast television, radio, and most popular magazines and newspapers. It is also an important contributor to big-time sports, concerts, and community events. An estimated $40 billion is spent per year on advertising in the United States alone, and similarly large expenditures characterize all developed economies.

Naturally, the decision makers who spend these vast sums are hungry for guidance. No one wants to spend millions of dollars on media purchases and hundreds of thousands making commercials only to find out that the targeted consumer did not notice, does not care, or worse yet, has become offended.

Advertising research generally attempts to measure or predict an awareness of an ad and its effectiveness. As the word implies, awareness is the degree to which the targeted consumers actually were exposed, or recall being exposed, to the advertising effort. This is frequently measured through some sort of media survey. Effectiveness measures change in consumer attitudes (such as perceptions that a particular product is of high quality or is "for me") or in behavior (increased foot traffic at car dealerships in response to a particular advertisement or campaign). Perceptual measures of effectiveness may be judged through either qualitative or quantitative means, while behavioral change is almost always measured quantitatively.

Promotions

Promotions include all sorts of nonadvertising activities that are designed to either increase awareness or stimulate trial of products. The most common of these are discounts, either trade discounts offered by manufacturers to retailers, or by couponing, rebating, or other discounts offered directly to consumers. Other promotions include direct experience of products and services, such as handing out free samples or allowing consumers to test the product. Still other promotions are designed merely to stimulate awareness or bring the consumer into contact with an opportunity to see or purchase the product—these include giveaways of merchandise bearing the product's name or image, as well as contests and sweepstakes. The common feature that unites all promotions and distinguishes them from advertising is that part of the expenditure goes directly to the consumer, either in the form of cash savings or merchandise or services.

Promotions usually are planned and executed in the same way as advertising campaigns and in many companies the same people will be involved. Research for promotions is also conducted along similar lines, with qualitative research dominating the design agenda and combinations of qualitative (usually focus groups) and quantitative (usually survey) methods being employed to evaluate promotional effectiveness.

Public Relations

Public relations activities are public actions and messages designed to create and nurture a positive image or aura around a particular company or product. They differ from advertising and promotions in that they do not generally involve direct statements of competitive benefits or characteristics. Typical public relations activities include sponsorship of community events, donations of money, equipment, or time to charities or communities, or other acts that the sponsor hopes will be interpreted as prosocial.

Large corporations almost always have a public relations department. Generally, this department is far removed from other marketing groups in the same company and populated by different people. In some cases, their efforts are completely autonomous and may even appear to be at odds with other marketing activities. The people who control budgets in these functions are less likely to have research experience than those in advertising or promotions. Most research surrounding public relations is straightforward opinion measurement, either qualitatively through focus groups or quantitatively through opinion surveys.

SALES MODELING AND PREDICTING

The end result of all marketing activities in the consumer behavior arena is sales, since these transactions are normally the only point at which revenue can actually pass from consumer to marketer. All businesses track sales as part of their normal accounting activities, so there is not much need for research in this area. However, businesses have almost as much interest in modeling and predicting future sales as they do in measuring those that have already occurred. Traditional ethnography as well as a variety of quantitative techniques that produce maps and models can be employed to these purposes.

At most companies, research concerning sales modeling and prediction will be the purview of the same department that handles marketing. Academic social scientists should be aware, however, that there is sometimes a rivalry, or even enmity, between the sales departments and marketing departments of a corporation. When budgets are available, these two groups may sometimes conduct competing research activities. The researcher should be cautious about being drawn into these battles, since siding with one party may permanently estrange you from ever working for the other.

Although there are a number of different aspects of sales modeling and prediction that are amenable to social science research methods, two topic areas account for the bulk of sales research projects. These two are purchase process and product introduction.

Purchase Process. One aspect of sales that receives a fair amount of research attention is the purchase process. Purchase process studies focus on the ways in which consumers formulate the decisions that ultimately lead them to purchase a particular product or service. Products that have long, complex decision processes (such as automobile purchase) or have high substitutability (such as snack foods or shampoos) are especially rich fields for purchase process studies. The aim of most purchase process research is to understand the key steps consumers (or a particular group of consumers) go through as they make their product choice. Knowing these steps and identifying sources of information or influence that consumers utilize at each step allow sellers to target their marketing activities more precisely.

Purchase process studies can utilize almost any qualitative or quantitative technique in the researcher's arsenal. Interview-based research, including ethnographic interviewing, can be particularly useful, especially if it is done "real time," as the person is actually making a product choice. For example, a study of female frequent clothing shoppers (those who shop for clothing at least several times per week and who purchase clothing at least once per week) might have an ethnographer do a "closet audit." The respondent would show her clothing collection to the ethnographer, whose questions would draw out the structure of such relevant dimensions as how the respondent puts outfits together, how she identifies a "gap" that would suggest a purchase, and the psychological and symbolic needs that are served by shopping for and purchasing clothes. In addition, the ethnographer might accompany the respondent on a shopping trip, interviewing and observing her as she examines, rejects, and selects purchases.

It is also common to ask purchase process questions during focus groups or in surveys. And multivariate statistical techniques, such as regression and conjoint analysis, have also been employed to quantify the role of particular variables in the purchase decision.

Product Introduction. No consumer-focused activity is more risky, from a financial perspective, than the introduction of a new product. This is especially true for products with lengthy, complex design and production cycles. A new model of automobile, for example, may represent up to $1 billion in design, development, tooling, and other costs before the first car rolls off the assembly line. A successful model may repay these costs many times over, but a failure will cost its manufacturer hundreds of millions of dollars. Even less costly products require substantial investment of manufacturing and marketing resources to get them in front of consumers.

Researchers new to the private sector should recognize that product introductions vary in their degree of newness. Some introductions are actually the creation of a new category of product. In these cases the marketing effort usually includes some element of explaining to the consumer what the heck the thing does, and why she needs it. An example in fairly recent memory is fax machines. Other introductions are radical combinations or repackaging of products that are already pretty familiar, for example, cellular phones. And others are minor variations on well established products (often referred to as product line extensions) such as double-stuffed Oreos.

Many product introduction studies are purely qualitative in nature, using focus groups or one-on-one interviews as the basis of data collection. And of course, the same multivariate techniques used in purchase process research can be used to project market response to a new product or service.

Public and Political Behavior

Another area in which commercial social science research is active is public and political behavior. Although the sums spent are not as massive as in consumer behavior, this is some of the most visible commercial research. Describing and predicting the attitudes and behavior of voters and the general citizenry is a mainstay of our public discourse (and an endless source of cocktail party chitchat). This highly visible field of social science research includes studies of public opinion, group action, and political behavior.

The constant presence of opinion polls in our news media, as well as endless poll analysis and predictions by pundits, indicates our national obsession with knowing and understanding what the neighbors think. There are a number of firms that specialize in public and political opinion polls, and almost all large market research firms are active in this area as well.

The most common method employed in researching public and political behavior is the ubiquitous opinion survey. In many cases the published findings do not go much beyond a straightforward presentation of the cross-tabbed percentages. But in some cases the need to fill additional air minutes or column inches or the desire to predict or influence behavior creates a market for more extensive research.

Using the same methods employed in market segmentation and targeting, survey data may be analyzed to identify groups or mind-sets that are of particular interest to the public discourse. The "soccer moms" prominently mentioned during the 1996 presidential race are an example of such a group. It is also common to supplement survey research with qualitative methods such as focus groups, which allow researchers to probe for the reasons behind the survey percentages. And of course, election coverage would not be complete without the statistical modeling that supports ever-earlier predictions of election outcomes.

Organizational Behavior

Private entities not only sponsor research to study their customers and the general public, they also occasionally will undertake research on themselves. Large companies have employee populations that exceed those of some cities, with the biggest numbering in the hundreds of thousands. Employees are the faces of the company to its markets, the hands behind its productive efforts, the minds behind its innovations, the consumers of its internal policies and programs, and the heart and soul of its corporate culture. Corporate executives and sometimes the stockholders and boards that direct them are anxious for tools to help manage the complex relationship between employer and employee (Ivancevich & Matteson, 1993).

For the most part, only larger employers (those with at least 1,000 employees) can afford the costs associated with hiring a social scientist to examine their organizations. Consequently, this field of commercial social science is much smaller than either consumer behavior or public behavior research. For those who find a niche in it, however, it can be extremely satisfying. In many ways, corporations are a kind of social science laboratory—organizations that are big enough and long-lasting enough to develop identifiable cultures but are directed enough to be subject to deliberate and thoughtful attempts at culture change. Executives may think they are running companies, but to the applied social scientist they are running great big experiments in anthropology, psychology, and sociology.

One of my clients provides a good illustration of this sort of real-life experiment. The client is a global firm consisting of more than 30 operating companies, mostly focused on some aspect of the construction and engineering business. It has more than 40,000 employees and works in approximately 50 countries. The company has a long history and both employees and executives feel that the company culture plays a role in its business success. Nevertheless, there is some sentiment that the culture must change in order to keep pace with the larger business environment, and company management has instituted a culture change initiative centered around six key values. Work with this client includes an ongoing series of measurements—are employees experiencing the values in action in the workplace? What barriers exist that keep the values from being fully implemented? Are there some groups or operating companies that are especially successful or less successful in implementing the values? These measurement activities include interviews with key informants, focus groups, and a periodic global opinion survey. In addition to measurement, we work with the client to design communications, policies, and programs to support and strengthen their values. To succeed, these programs must be sensitive not only to the client's goals, but to the existing culture—a program that might work in another organization could be a complete flop in this one. Because our work with this client is long-term, we get the opportunity to see the results of their culture change efforts as they occur (or fail to occur).

Naturally, companies are concerned about the attitudes and behavior of their employees. Good employee morale can translate into lower turnover and recruitment costs, higher productivity and innovation, lower costs for employer-paid health care and workmen's compensation, less threat of strikes, and avoidance of employee-sponsored lawsuits. In addition to these bottom-line considerations, many business leaders desire the good opinion of their employees or at least wish to avoid presiding over their collective misery. In consequence, many large companies at least sporadically attempt to assess how their employees are thinking, feeling, and behaving.

Research projects involving employee populations generally focus on one of two levels. The first is the overall morale or climate survey. Typically quantitative, these projects attempt to assess how employees feel in relation to a number of issues deemed important to the company's well-being. Firms that conduct such studies often field them every year or two and pay particular attention to changes over time. In contrast, other studies are tactical in nature, focusing on particular programs or policies such as benefits, compensation, performance management, or internal communications. Depending on the particular research objective, these projects may be either qualitative (most typically using focus groups) or quantitative in method. But whether they focus on overall morale or on policies and programs, the primary aim of these studies is to help executives and managers prioritize their efforts and resources.

The business world is full of talk about corporate cultures, and anyone who has had exposure to more than a few big companies will attest to their existence and variety. In some cases, executives may go beyond the usual morale or program assessments to really examine their corporate culture. Most often these studies are a response to some significant change: a merger, an acquisition, a layoff, rapid growth, new management, or a perceived change in the business environment. These studies, although rare, allow the researcher a chance to use the entire range of ethnographic tools, as well as to engage the substantial literature on change and change management (Bridges, 1988; Hampden-Turner & Trompenaars, 1993).

4. MARKETING YOURSELF
TO THE PRIVATE SECTOR

A researcher who wishes to be employed in the private sector must make potential clients and employers aware of her existence and capabilities. Although this chapter is primarily aimed at those who wish to work on the supplier side (since they must market continuously), those targeting client side jobs may find many of the same techniques useful in attracting the attention of potential employers and building a resume for the climb up the corporate ladder.

Visibility

One of the most critical elements in getting hired in the private sector is visibility. In researching a particular industry or potential employer you may have already achieved some visibility, attending industry functions, visiting industry or company hangouts, making contacts, and arranging informational interviews. Several other activities can further increase your visibility and credibility with your desired business audience. These activities include teaching, public speaking, getting press in print and electronic media, and public relations activities.

Teaching a class can be an excellent way to demonstrate your expertise and work style. To be a useful path to private-sector employment, however, it is vital that the class be taught to an audience that contains potential employers or at least those with direct contacts to potential employers. The undergraduate and graduate students found in most university classrooms do not meet this criterion (at least not in the short term). But many communities do offer teaching opportunities with greater career potential. Extension or evening courses aimed at adult, mid-career businesspeople are where you should position yourself. Design or adapt a course that you believe fits with the needs and interests of your target audience and which will allow you to showcase your talents. If you have expertise or entree to a particular ethnic group, you might consider teaching a course called "Inside the Minds of Hispanic Consumers" or "Connecting With Your Black Customers." Aim to attract the sort of people who control or influence research budgets—mid-to-high-level marketers, human resources managers. or advertisers. Do not neglect to give it a catchy title—you want it to stand out in the course catalog. Then approach the gatekeepers of the local university, college, and school district adult education programs. With luck you will find a program that needs additional courses and is willing to put yours into their schedule. You can also see if there is a need for additional instructors or sessions for established courses that appear to draw the right audience and for which you are appropriately qualified.

In many ways, visibility-enhancing public speaking is just like teaching a class, except that the entire class is reduced to just a single session. The gatekeepers for public speaking opportunities are business, trade, and community groups (local American Marketing Association chapters are especially useful and are always looking for speakers). When you research business and industry trade associations, you should always be alert for those that need speakers for their meetings and trade shows. If a group seems interested in having you as a speaker, be sure to ask a few screening questions to make sure you will not be wasting your time talking to the wrong audience. Are the people who will be in attendance from the correct industries? How senior are they? What roles do they play in their companies? What do they expect from a speaker? Can you hand out promotional materials? Can you collect business cards or get a roster of attendees? Will the event be publicized? Will they pay you? At least feed you? If you secure a public-speaking opportunity with a desirable audience be sure to give them a blow-their-socks-off performance. Treat all public speeches as you would treat a final project results presentation for your most important client. After all, your most important client (or client to be) may actually be in the audience.

Getting quoted or interviewed by the press is one of the most entertaining ways of becoming visible. It is a lot of fun to see or hear yourself described as an expert, and it generally does not take much time or preparation (it also impresses the hell out of relatives who always thought you spent all that time in school just to avoid getting a real job). This method is especially useful for researchers who are witty, highly verbal, photogenic, or personally interesting and entertaining. It should be approached more cautiously (but not necessarily discarded) by those who like to speak from a prepared script, or who are easily flustered.

Getting media exposure is usually a combination of effort and luck. General interest newspapers, magazines, and news bureaus keep lists of expert contacts in many fields When they need a quote or commentary for an article, the writer or support staff will just start dialing numbers of likely "experts." Those who are immediately available are the ones who get quoted. Lists of experts are often casually compiled and there is no surefire way to secure a listing. A method that works in some cases is to send press releases of your most interesting and career-relevant research findings. This has some chance of putting you in the expert file, and if it is a slow news day, may even result in a small article or short interview. You will probably have your best results with business or industry journals, especially the smaller and more specialized ones. These publications are often short of interesting material to fill their pages, and they are often willing to provide you with some exposure in exchange for a usable article or interview (See Appendix B for an example of a press release). Just call the editor or editorial assistant of your targeted publication and test the waters. If they ask you to write an article, consider taking payment (if any is offered—or even if it is not) in advertising space. This can be an inexpensive way to combine advertising with visibility activities.

The final category of visibility activities is public relations. Researchers new to the private sector may think that PR is something done only by big companies with megabudgets (or mega-image problems). Not true. There are numerous public relations activities that are appropriate for individuals or small business concerns. If you are currently involved with community or charitable groups as a sponsor or volunteer, you can use your involvement as a PR opportunity. Put your donation in your business name, wear a T-shirt with your business logo to volunteer functions, or otherwise become a professional rather than just individual contributor. Remember that not all groups and activities are appropriate forums for commercial sponsorship, and that not all your potential clients will share your preferences regarding worthy social causes. If you apply common sense, you will probably find that some of your good works provide worthwhile PR opportunities. And if making a commercial link encourages or enables you to increase your charitable contributions, so much the better.

Capabilities Presentations—Content

Once a potential client has been identified and has indicated a willingness to learn more about a researcher's services, a capabilities presentation should be scheduled. This presentation serves two purposes: skills presentation and relationship building. The presentation allows both the researcher and the client to assess whether there is a good fit between the client's research needs and the researcher's capabilities. A well-constructed capabilities presentation will address the following issues.

THE KINDS OF BUSINESS PROBLEMS YOU CAN HELP SOLVE

Potential clients view research as a means to achieving their business goals. Either through prepresentation research or in your initial contacts with potential clients, you should learn how they characterize the problems facing their businesses. Your presentation should echo this characterization, making clear that you understand their issues and that you are offering a means of at least partly resolving their problems. This approach engages the client's interest and assures her that you understand her business.

THE METHODS YOU USE

You should describe your methodological expertise in terms that are clear, succinct, and free of scientific jargon. The level of detail should be appropriate to the audience. The high-school-educated CEO of a firm considering its first research purchase will probably appreciate a brief explanation of your methods, but will not enjoy an overly detailed academic dissertation on the finer points of obscure theoretical constructs. In contrast, a research manager with a social science PhD may require a very precise description of exactly what methods and techniques you intend to use and may wish to engage in active debate about the pros and cons of alternative approaches. In every capabilities presentation, there is the risk of losing your audience, either by talking over their heads, or by insultingly underestimating their knowledge or sophistication. In general, brevity is the best way to avoid these pitfalls. Those audience members who want more detail about methods should be able to get their answers during questions and answers rather than during the body of the presentation itself.

WHAT KINDS OF PRODUCT YOU DELIVER

In order to put you on the bid list, a potential client must have a clear idea of the form and format of your research output. Will there be a written report, a live presentation of results, audio or video tapes, transcripts, questionnaires, data files or tapes? Most audiences will consider the capabilities presentation itself to be a demonstration of your presentation style and document production, so it is important that both verbal and written content accurately reflect what you can (and will) do under real-world time and budget constraints.

EVIDENCE OF COMPETENCE AND EXPERIENCE

In addition to understanding what you do and how you do it, potential clients need to be convinced that you do it well and that you are not a research novice hoping to self-educate with the client's money. For most clients, the most compelling evidence of competence is similar work done for a previous (and satisfied) client. Audiences vary widely as to what they will count as "similar." For some, all you need to show is that you have successful experience with the methodology. Others will only be comfortable with a demonstration that you have previously addressed the exact same research problem for an almost identical firm, preferably one of the client's close competitors. Most are somewhere in the middle and will want to see some sort of profile of the researcher's background and credentials, descriptions or demonstrations of previous research, and a client list. Most of this material should be in written or electronic (i.e., tapes of interviews or focus groups) form, left behind with the client rather than presented verbally. The verbal presentation itself, of course, should be focused on the demonstration of competence and familiarity with the client's issues and ways of addressing them.

WHY YOU ARE A BETTER CHOICE THAN THE COMPETITION

It is important to remember that the goal of the capabilities presentation is not just to show that you are good, but that you are superior to other choices that may be available. This may be a superiority of the proposed research over other things that a potential client might spend her money on, or superiority over other researchers and their methods. This is sometimes a difficult concept for researchers coming from academia, where competition is masked (at least most of the time) by polite social forms offering the pleasant delusion that research and researchers are evaluated on their intrinsic merits. A capabilities presentation that convinces a client that research is needed should also leave no doubt as to who the best researcher for the job might be. Clients need to know the basis of your competitive advantage, so do not be afraid to list explicitly the benefits of using your services. Are you faster, cheaper, more experienced, more methodologically sophisticated, more in tune with their problems or industry, more convenient to work with, a better writer or presenter, a more meticulous researcher, more innovative, or more personable? Most of the decision makers who control research funds must justify their spending choices to their superiors. Your capabilities presentation should provide them with plenty of support for their choice to hire you.

Capabilities Presentations—Context

While your presentation provides the potential client with the information to decide rationally whether or not to use your services, it is important to recognize that few business decisions are made on a purely rational basis. Consequently, it is important that the capabilities presentation not neglect more human elements that often make the difference between being seen as competent and actually getting on the list of bidders for the next project. These elements include the following:

ADDRESSING THE RIGHT PEOPLE

It is important to learn who actually controls the research budget at a potential client firm, as well as who has influence on that decision maker. At small companies spending decisions may be made at the CEO level; this is especially true if the company is a closely held private firm. At big companies, the budgets are controlled by middle managers. In general, those who influence budget decisions are not more than one level above or below the actual decision maker. When you schedule a capabilities presentation you should do everything in your power to make sure you are dealing with decision makers and influence wielders. It is better to present one-on-one to a decision maker than to a roomful of interested but peripheral parties.

PRESENTATION TIMING AND LENGTH

The most standard time length for capabilities presentations is about one hour. Be sure that your presentation does not completely fill the scheduled time slot. It is common for presentations to start a few minutes late, as audience members may be coming from other meetings or may need to be tracked down and reminded of the presentation. In addition, you should allow adequate time for questions and answers at the end of the presentation. No client ever objects to a presentation that ends a few minutes early, but many will get quite irritated at one that runs over. If the questions and answers period threatens to run over time, be sure to give those who need to leave an opportunity to do so gracefully. This is especially important if the questions are all coming from one person or a small group. If there seems to be a lot of postpresentation interest from key decision makers, it may be best to schedule a follow-up meeting to specifically address their questions. This serves the combined function of answering questions and giving you another opportunity for client contact. Remember that you want to leave the potential client eager to see more of you, not irritated by your imposition on his time.

While length is a primary issue in capabilities presentations, timing can also be important. Most businesses have both seasonal and weekly cycles of workflow, as well as all-important budgeting cycles. Use your contacts in the client firm to learn the best timing for your presentation. Issues you should consider include convenience for key decision makers, upcoming decision deadlines that may require the research, and client traditions about the proper or best time for vendor presentations.

STYLE AND TONE

You should be able to tailor your presentation to each potential client. Once again, you should thoroughly interview any contacts you have at the potential client firm. Some firms (or groups within firms) are very conservative in dress and manner (this is often true in financial services companies), whereas others, such as advertising firms, are so free-wheeling as to be downright wacky. If it is possible to visit the client firm before your presentation (perhaps by inviting your contact to lunch) you should seize this opportunity. Observe the office layout (enclosed offices or open workstations), decor (both corporate and the personal touches added by employees), employee interactions, and emphasis (or lack thereof) on hierarchy. A good rule of thumb is to mimic the look and tone of either the key decision makers or their immediate superiors. Do not, however, allow your mimicry to descend into cheap caricature.

Documents and presentation decks (the collection of overhead transparencies or slides that support the presentation) may also be customized to the client's style. This can be done most precisely if you get to see reports of previous research (especially those the client thought were well done) or one of the client's internal reports or presentations. If possible, make your materials somewhat better in look and quality than those the client is used to. If the client's document production capabilities are really primitive, be careful that you do not go too far. Some conservative firms see glitzy presentations and reports as a triumph of form over substance and will be suspicious of the quality of the research (the author once heard a disgruntled client describe an over-produced report by sneering "I reviewed the document and found it very . . . pretty").

SCHMOOZING AND FOLLOW-UP

Unless the client has a project immediately available for bidding, the capabilities presentation will not instantly result in your being hired. It is important to keep your name and capabilities fresh in the client's mind until the opportunity to bid for a specific project arrives. This will require periodic follow-up. A number of methods are available to maintain client contact. The most common and least costly is the occasional telephone call to see if the client has any upcoming projects that might require your services. Like the capabilities presentation itself, these calls should be scheduled with an awareness of the client's project-planning cycle. In most cases calls more frequent than once every month or two will seem irritating to potential clients. In contrast, calling only once or twice a year is likely to cause you to miss the planning stages of many projects. You should adjust your call frequency to maximize your chance of getting bid opportunities without exceeding the client's tolerance level.

Another popular method of maintaining client contact is to publish a newsletter relating to interesting tidbits from your research. Newsletters are a powerful marketing device and are commonly used by large research firms. A newsletter keeps your name in front of clients and allows you to demonstrate your expertise on an ongoing basis. An effective newsletter must be informative and interesting enough that clients and prospects will want to read it. Before launching a newsletter, it is important to evaluate whether you have sufficient material of this sort to support an ongoing publication, and if you wish to commit to the deadlines associated with a regular publishing schedule in addition to other work demands. Newsletters are most feasible for those who do at least some of their work in nonconfidential settings or who have clients who want particular research results publicized. This technique is especially effective when the newsletter topics are suitable for consumption by client company spokespeople who must speak to the press. These people are always looking for timely information that they can turn into quotes or sound bites. Clients are often happy to get such newsletters, and you get the added benefit of appearing to be an expert on the newsletter topic. An Internet home page is a cost-effective alternative to a newsletter for those who have the appropriate interest and skills.

Most research firms, especially the larger ones, put some of their client contact efforts into schmoozing. Usually this takes the form of inviting clients out for meals, to sporting events, to receptions and cocktail parties, or presenting them with gifts. Client firms and decision makers vary widely in their policies and reactions to these activities. Almost all client firms have anticorruption policies that restrict the sorts of items and benefits that their employees may accept from vendors. Enforcement of these policies, however, varies widely. In general, client personnel are allowed to accept normal business meals or small promotional items such as coffee cups, desk accessories, or calendars. Some companies also allow their personnel to accompany vendors to entertainment, golf outings, or sporting events, but many forbid this practice. Outright gifts are usually forbidden and smack of bribery. Try to learn the policies and customs of your potential clients before engaging in these activities. And of course, make sure that the cost of schmoozing does not exceed your budget for marketing activities.

Promotional Materials

Before and between visits and phone calls, promotional materials are your means of contact with potential clients. The variety and scale of these materials should be appropriate to your marketing budget and types of clients you plan to approach. The major categories of promotional materials are described below:

TRASH AND TRINKETS

A popular category of promotional materials is small items meant to be left behind after a visit to a client. These items should be informative, attention-grabbing, and distinctive. All items should carry your name or company logo, and wherever appropriate your telephone number and address. Promotional goods of this type are sometimes referred to as "trash and trinkets," and there is a sizable industry that produces and sells these goodies. The commonest items are wearables (T-shirts, hats, etc.), office accessories (calendars, computer mouse pads, coasters, pens, clocks, pencil holders, address books, etc.), and small toys.

The most effective promotional materials are those that have high utility (so the client hangs on to them), are unique (so they do not get buried among all the other trash in the office), are attractive (so they are used a lot or kept in visible locations), and in which the item is somehow related to the vendor's product or service (e.g., if you sell beer, give out bottle openers).

BUSINESS CARDS

The most important thing about business cards is to have them. Have plenty of them and do not go anywhere without them. Almost everyone in the business world keeps a file of business cards, so these will be your most enduring promotional materials. Naturally, business cards should be well-printed on good-quality stock. Stick to standard sizes and formats; odd-sized cards are likelier to be lost or overlooked. The card should not be too busy, but should also not be so stingy with information as to create room for confusion about who you are or what you do. Avoid cute. Keep to the basics; your name, title, company name or logo, address, e-mail address, phone and fax numbers.

LETTERHEAD

A letterhead is not a necessity for a small freelance operation, but adds a nice touch if the revenue justifies it. If you do not have a letterhead for your business, plain white or ivory paper is the best choice. If you have an academic position that supplies a letterhead, be cautious about using it for business purposes. In general, if your activities are sanctioned by your academic employer, use of a letterhead is okay. If not, it is theft. Potential clients may also be concerned about your use of university letterhead for nonacademic activities, reasoning that your tendency to be free with your employer's property may extend to any resources they would put at your command during a research project.

The design of your letterhead should be client friendly and informative. Choice of stock, colors, layout and typeface should be in keeping with the kind of impression you wish to convey to clients: conservative vs. innovative, academic vs. business, fun vs. serious. Information on the letterhead should be similar to that on your business cards, along with a logo or motto if appropriate.

BROCHURES

Like letterheads, brochures are needed only when revenue justifies the expense. There is considerable room for creativity in design of brochures. They may be die-cut, single or double-folded, stapled or bound. Printing may be single or multicolor, graphics may be used, and a huge variety of stocks and finishes are available. As with a letterhead, the key issue in designing the brochure is the impression you wish to leave with its readers. The key difference is that in a brochure you have the opportunity to use text and pictures in a relatively extensive way to make that impression. Elements commonly included in researcher brochures are the following:

Descriptions and listing of areas of expertise
Case studies and testimonials
Client list
Personnel biographies

PRESENTATION DECKS

It is common to leave copies of presentation decks with those who attend the presentation. Be sure to have hard copies ready for this purpose. If you are presenting at a client company, these hard copies should be handed out after the presentation. If you present at an association or other semipublic setting, collect the business cards of interested parties and send the hard copies the next day. This technique allows you to build a file of interested contacts and gives you the means and the excuse for follow-up conversation.

5. PROJECT MANAGEMENT

The Contract Process

For most social scientists coming from academia, a substantial hurdle to private sector practice is the contract process. Although this shares some characteristics with pursuing an academic grant, the norms are sufficiently different to warrant a brief description here.

THE RFP

Most social science research in the private sector is (at least nominally) put out for competitive bids. A new researcher or research firm will almost always get their first job with a client by winning in a competitive bid situation. All the activities associated with promoting your services are designed to get on the list of bidders. This activity culminates when a potential client provides a Request for Proposal or Request for Bid (usually referred to in the research world as an RFP).

An RFP may be anything from a verbal request outlining the research objectives to a 50-page document specifying the exact form, length, and content of acceptable bids. Normally, the RFP will have some sort of list of objectives, at least a general description of the type of research the client has in mind, and a deadline for submission of bids (Appendix A contains a sample RFP).

The most important thing about an RFP is to read it carefully. It is vital that you understand what the client really wants and that you prepare your bid accordingly. If the RFP is unclear, call the party who issued it and ask some questions. In fact, if you do not have any real questions, make some up and call anyway. This will give you a chance to probe for underlying issues that might not be visible in the RFP. It also gives you a chance to listen to the client's vocabulary, language you should consider parroting back in your bid. And of course, every call is an opportunity to bond with the client, demonstrating your technical expertise, deep understanding of their needs, professionalism and charm.

BID CONSTRUCTION AND SUBMISSION

Private-sector research bids range from one-page memos to book-length bound documents with slick covers, fancy graphics, and professional art design. If possible you should learn what your client expects. If you have a close relationship with your client contact, you can ask to view previous winning bids. At the very least you can interview the client about her expectations.

Bids that are only a few pages long are generally written in letter format or as an attachment to a brief cover letter. Longer documents are more likely to be bound—anything that is more than 10 pages, especially if it contains one or more sections that are more than two pages long, is a candidate for binding. Regardless of length, bids typically contain the following sections:

Background (optional): States the context of the study.

Objectives: This is the "why."

Approach (Method or Methodology): Describes "what, where and how."

Schedule (Timing): Describes "when."

Deliverables: Lists what the client will get—videotapes, audiotapes, transcripts, translations, discussion guides, questionnaires, data processing, interviewing, moderating, recruiting, facility rental, cross-tabulations, multivariate statistics, analysis, descriptions, projections, conclusions, recommendations, reports, presentations, consultation, and so on.

Fees (Costs or Estimated Fees): This is the "how much." Be sure you include everything the client is expected to pay for; either build it into your overall fee or provide an itemized list. Do not forget things like travel expenses, printing and duplicating, postage, and so on.

Biographies (optional): This is the "who" and should mention aspects of your history that are relevant to the proposed work. Do not drone on too long, it is easy for a "who" to turn into a "who cares?"

List of clients (optional): Use only if they are impressive. Be careful about listing the client's direct competitors. Some will be thrilled that you have experience with their industry, others will be concerned that you will carry confidential information from one to the other.

Attachments (optional): These can be examples that illustrate things the client might find easier to see than to read about; possible items include graphical presentations of multivariate output, questionnaire formats, and so on. If you show examples of output, do not show anything that identifies a previous client—give it a fictitious name and dummy up the data. You do not want clients to think that you might run around showing their data to strangers.

BID PRESENTATIONS

For large projects you may be asked or allowed to submit your bid in the form of a presentation. A bid presentation is usually in addition to, rather than instead of, the written bid document. In most cases a bid presentation means that the entire panel of decision makers will be in the room, waiting to be impressed by your professionalism and technical ability.

For most bid presentations, you will prepare a presentation deck of overhead transparencies. Some client facilities may also allow you to use slides or computer-generated decks. But transparencies are the standard, and fancier presentation methods should only be used when you are certain that they will function smoothly and have the desired impact. Be sure to bring hard copies of your presentation deck with you and give one to each attendee so they can take notes. If the group is small and friendly you may choose to ditch the transparencies in favor of the greater intimacy of simply leading the group through the deck together.

Whatever its form, the presentation deck should highlight key elements of your proposal. You may also use the presentation to demonstrate aspects of your bid that distinguish you from other vendors; for example, exercises you plan to use with the research participants, clever ways of presenting the data, and the like. Make the presentation an appealing experience for the client; use interesting visuals, props, or exercises that involve them. Use humor, as well, providing you can carry it off without offending the client or portraying yourself as frivolous.

In most cases you should encourage client questions during the presentation. Clients who are asking questions are staying with you and are likelier to form a good impression of you. Most people love to talk and get bored when someone else talks too long. If clients want to speak, let 'em. Also be sure to leave some time at the end of your allotted presentation period for more questions and answers and general discussion.

Be sure to have a strong conclusion to your presentation. Remind the clients of your strengths and reiterate your desire to work with them. Opportunities to have direct contact with clients during the decision process are rare and valuable, so make the most of them.

BID REVIEWING

The bid review process is as variable as the form and format of RFPs. In some cases a single person may make the decision, in others it will be a group decision—not necessarily one in which each party has an equal vote.

48

Some companies habitually accept the lowest bid that seems of adequate quality. Others use complex formulas that rate different aspects of each bid and then weight them into a final answer. Many use some sort of spreadsheet or matrix in which to record ratings or comments. Many others are just a consensus "gut feel" in which the reviewers just talk themselves to a decision. You should always attempt to learn how your bid will be reviewed and who will be involved in the process and tailor your work accordingly.

Deliverables

Marketing is promising to deliver. Work is delivering what you promise.

Although marketing yourself is the key to beginning a private sector career, it is the quality and content of the work itself that most determines if that career will continue and flourish. No one will pay you (at least not more than once) for your marketing efforts. It is imperative that you deliver fully on your contracted services. And as with all your other activities, you must translate and acculturate your notions of work into terms that are recognizable and coherent to private sector participants. Your deliverables form the primary basis of the private sector's perception of who you are and what you do.

DOCUMENTS

Most deliverables in private-sector research are documents, typically reports of findings. Unlike academic articles, in which content and format are rigidly specified by editorial style sheets, private-sector reports of findings offer considerable room for creativity. The only firm guidelines are that the document should convey the key information to the reader in a user-friendly way.

There are, of course, some norms regarding reports of findings. Results may be presented in summary or at length, in text, in graphics, or in both. In general, qualitative findings, such as reports of focus group interviews, are presented in one of three standard lengths—the "topline" which presents an overview of key findings in a one-to-five page format, the "summary report" which summarizes the research in 10 to 20 pages, and a "full report" which reports every relevant finding and may run to 100 pages or more. Some projects may require both a topline and one of the more extensive formats, since a topline is often used in situations such as product tests or copy or advertising testing in which some decision needs to be made immediately. In these cases the topline, focusing just on those issues relevant to the pending decision, will be written within one or two days of the conclusion of data collection and delivered immediately to the client. The longer report, which usually will include findings on a somewhat broader range of issues, will be written and delivered a week or so later.

Reports of quantitative findings are also delivered in a wide range of report formats. Most typically, these reports include an executive summary of a few pages. Typical contents in an executive summary would be Objectives, Methodology, Participant Profile, Key Findings, and Conclusions and Recommendations. Following the executive summary (sometimes as a separate document) will be the detailed findings. These would include text descriptions and graphic and or numerical displays of all relevant data. Depending on the norms of the client, text may be in either paragraph or bullet point form. Supporting documents such as copies of questionnaires, discussion guides, sampling schemes, and the like are included in an appendix.

DATA

Items in a number of categories qualify as data. If your project is primarily qualitative, the data produced may include audio- or videotapes, transcripts of focus groups or interviews, photographs, field notes, and the like. For quantitative work, the data may include questionnaires, paper books of tabulated data, and electronic data files.

The disposition of data varies by project and client. In many cases, clients do not wish to have direct possession of their data. This is especially true for clients who have no in-house analytical capability or in projects for which the data will quickly become obsolete. Others simply do not want to be bothered with storing and organizing something that they will not use frequently or are simply content to have the report of findings and nothing else. Others will want everything.

Be sure that expectations about the types and dispositions of data are clear to all parties. Do not allow for any uncertainties; ownership of research materials is a potentially contentious issue that can lead to broken relationships or even lawsuits. If you are handing materials over to clients, make sure there is a mutual understanding about whether or not you may keep copies, what you can or cannot do with those copies, and how long you will guarantee to have copies in your possession. If the client does not take possession, be clear about what you are keeping, how long you will keep it, whether or not you can access the materials for nonclient purposes, and how it will be disposed of at the end of the archiving period.

For most projects the simplest method is to hand over all agreed-upon materials immediately after receiving full payment. If you are acting as archivist, send the client a separate notice stating what you are archiving, how long the archive will be preserved, and what your rights and the client's rights are to the material. If you archive client materials for lengthy periods, it is a good idea to contact them again at the end of the archive period and reconfirm that they are willing to let you destroy the materials.

PRESENTATIONS

Upon completion of the project, it is common for the researcher to present the results in person, often handing over the written copies of the report at the same time. For a small project, this presentation might be quite informal, basically just a sit-down with your client contact in which you walk them through the highlights of the report. For a major project, a presentation might be much more formal, and the audience might include high-ranking members of the client firm.

Formal presentations of results should be handled in much the way you would handle a bid presentation or capabilities presentation. Be very aware of client norms and expectations; if you have been working with them for weeks or months, there's no excuse for being ignorant. Make sure that your materials are informative, clear, complete, and appealing. Allow plenty of time for questions and answers; clients can get very excited about their own data. And if some of your findings are apt to be controversial or threatening to part of the audience, be ready to respond professionally and without getting angry or flustered.

CONCLUSIONS AND RECOMMENDATIONS

Some projects end with a presentation of findings. In these cases the client will simply take your data and make of them what they will. In other cases, the client will expect you to draw conclusions from the data and perhaps to recommend a course of action. The most important factor in making conclusions and recommendations is not to go further than your knowledge of the client's situation and business will allow. Doing a detailed ethnography of athletic shoe purchase patterns does not make you an expert on the casual clothing industry; in contrast, your client probably *is* an expert. Stick to conclusions that are drawn directly from the data. If possible do not make recommendations unless you can kick them around first with knowledgeable client contacts. Nothing is more embarrassing than suggesting a course of action that the client or his direct competitor has already tried and failed at.

6. BUSINESS MANAGEMENT

"Fast, cheap or good. Pick any two."

—The fundamental law of business.

Perhaps the biggest barrier encountered by academics who wish to enter the private sector is their real or perceived ignorance of business management. The vast literature on starting and running a business, along with frightening statistics on business failures and corporate layoffs, can make the private sector look very dangerous. But in reality, most of business management can be divided into three simple areas: client management, time management, and money management. For the most part, the skills required in each of these areas parallel those in academic life and are well within the reach of most social scientists.

Client Management

Managing clients is similar to managing any other human relationship (in other words, impossible). The skills you use in your academic and personal life to keep colleagues, friends, and family on your side are identical to those you will need in the private sector. This section will not belabor those points. Rather it will focus on three areas where private-sector norms of client management differ somewhat from those found in academic or personal settings. These areas are communications, confidentiality, and conflict management.

COMMUNICATIONS

No one would dispute the key role of communications in managing and mediating any human relationship. But in the private sector, communications are even more crucial. Even though all relationships have aspects that are similar to legal contracts, the relationship between client and researcher is explicitly contractual. This contractual framework means that messages communicated between parties may easily take on the status of legal obligations and that misunderstandings are potentially subject to litigation. To

52

avoid these negative consequences, it is essential than communications with clients be clear, complete, and frequent.

In the contractual setting, clarity means *mutual* understanding. It is not enough for you to know what you are going to do and how you are going to do it. The client must also share that understanding. A client who does not understand is likely to be surprised, and there are no pleasantly surprised clients. Every communication with a client, be it verbal or written, should include some elements that confirm understanding. For example, an e-mail note or memo can include a summary of previously agreed points or an explicit statement of intended next steps. Verbal contacts should also end with some sort of checkpoint that confirms understanding and intentions. If you make these checkpoints a regular part of your communications, you are much less likely to confront a surprised and angry client.

It is equally important that researcher/client communications be complete. Never assume that you are burdening the client with too much information or excessive detail. Err on the side of more-than-they-need-to-know. Your client contacts may have conversations about your project with others whom you never see. If your client is asked a question about your project, he may "fill in the blanks" to cover areas of ignorance, especially if he is grilled by someone of higher ranking. If you give him the information to answer correctly, you'll never have to help him backpedal out of one of these awkward situations. It is true that there are "dead times" during many projects, but do not neglect communications during these times. The client wants to know what's going on, even if nothing much is happening. Provide regular progress reports. Frequent contact keeps clients calm and well-informed.

CONFIDENTIALITY AND SECURITY

Academic norms support the sharing of research results. In fact in most fields, results are not officially "yours" unless and until they have been shared with colleagues in a published paper or presentation at a professional forum. Academic research is generally carried out in a very public fashion, with no attempt to conceal the existence or direction of the study. And most data from academic studies have little or no market value and are not in danger of sabotage or theft.

These norms contrast sharply with the private sector, in which research results are regarded as the very valuable personal property of the sponsoring party. In addition, many of the conversations that are needed to conduct commercial research require that clients reveal information that could be very damaging to the client or useful to its competitors if made public. Failure to observe private-sector norms of confidentiality and security can not only destroy your relationships with clients, it can lead to financially disastrous litigation. If you want to employ your skills in the private sector you must observe its conventions of confidentiality and security.

All communications with clients, whether written, electronic, or verbal, should be treated as confidential. If you need to share information about a client with others (e.g., when seeking the professional services of subcontractors or advisers) either conceal the identity of the client or ask the other party to keep the information confidential. If extensive exchanges of data or documents are required, do not hesitate to ask vendors to sign a simple confidentiality agreement. Similarly, if your client asks you to sign a confidentiality agreement, review it and (assuming it is reasonable in wording and extent) sign it.

Both your research findings and materials provided to you by clients may represent considerable financial value. Inappropriate exposure of this material to competitors, the press, or the public can be trouble for your client and in the case of big dollar projects such as new product launches, can put millions of dollars in investment at risk. And rest assured that if your client suffers because of your carelessness, her corporate attorneys will see to it that she does not suffer alone. Taking reasonable security measures is the best way to stay out of court.

Industrial espionage does occur, but only a small percentage of security breaches are due to actual theft or deliberate eavesdropping. If information falls into the wrong hands, it is generally because of poor document handling or careless conversation. If your office is in a location that is not fully secure, be sure to have a place in your office (such as a locking file drawer) that is. Do not leave confidential materials lying around when you are not present. If visitors enter your office while you are working with confidential materials, put them away or at least turn the documents face down. Many researchers also use caution in labeling documents so that outsiders cannot easily guess the topic and contents—this rule applies both to hard copy and electronic files.

Travel represents a special category of security risks. A shocking number of documents is left in airports, on planes, in rental vehicles, and in hotels. Others disappear when luggage is lost or stolen. The general rule is to keep all confidential materials with you or in a hotel safe. If you work on airplanes or in airports, do not put documents in seat-back pockets or nearby seats. Keep documents in briefcases or luggage that fastens, not in outside open pockets or open bookbags. Do not spread documents all over your hotel room or other temporary workspace. Avoid checking your luggage on the airplane or leaving it in a rental car. Just assume that all confidential documents have legs and will run away if you give them a chance.

Conversations also represent security risks. You should always be very aware not only of whom you are talking to but who is close enough to overhear. Take particular care during conversations on airplanes, in elevators, and in restaurants. If you are speaking with clients or colleagues in such public spaces (you would presumably not discuss your client's business with anyone else), try to adjust your conversation to make eavesdropping harder and less productive. For example, you can refer to projects by code names or nicknames and shy away from mentioning specific dates, dollar figures, or outcomes. Even if your client seems oblivious to security risks, be as cautious as is reasonably possible. Just because the client behaves carelessly does not mean he will not object to your doing likewise.

CONFLICT RESOLUTION

As in any other human endeavor, conflicts arise in the course of conducting private-sector research. Because private-sector research often concerns matters involving confidential information and large sums of money, conflicts can lead to ruined reputations, loss of business, and even litigation. It is therefore vital to have some plan in mind to deal with conflicts.

Naturally, the best conflict resolution is conflict prevention. It is impossible to overemphasize the role of clear, complete, and explicit communications in this regard. When appropriate, put agreements and expectations in writing and get the signature or explicit verbal agreement of your client contact for all decisions about budgets, courses of action, deliverables and deadlines. Be clear and honest with research participants about what you expect from them and how the information they provide will be used. Reconfirm your understanding and planned next steps at each contact. Do not make any assumptions about what they expect (ask 'em) and do not let them make assumptions about what you will do (tell 'em). Most conflicts occur when clients are surprised, so make it your business to seek out and destroy surprises before they hatch.

If you should get into a conflict with a client, approach it in a businesslike (rather than emotional) way. Key elements to consider during client/vendor conflicts include the magnitude of the problem, division of responsibility for the problem, the value of the client's future business with you, the amount of harm the client might do your business if he remains angry, the probability of saving the relationship, and the material and psychological cost required to save it. Consider all these factors long and well before you choose a course of action. Although it is true that not all client relationships can be saved, and not all are worth saving, it is even more true that in the entire history of business, no one has ever, ever, ever actually won an argument with a client.

Should you choose to appease an unhappy client, either because you are at fault or because appeasement makes better business sense than pointing out to the client how he's at fault, you will use one or both of the following two main categories of appeasement techniques:

Stage One Appeasement: Apology/Groveling

Say how sorry you are. Say it sincerely. Say it several times. Explain what you are going to do to see that something like this never happens again. Remind them how much you value their business and their good opinion. State your hope that this unfortunate incident has not marred an otherwise beautiful professional relationship. When they assure you that it has not, smile joyfully, express your relief, and shut up. Never mention the conflict again.

Stage Two Appeasement: When Words Are Not Enough

If you really are at fault, you should be prepared to make good on your errors. Normally this will be handled as a discount on services. You may either discount the services in dispute or offer a discount on future services. The second course is preferable, since it presumes a continuing client/vendor relationship. However, if your errors have cost a client time, money or market opportunity, a discount on the current service is probably in order. You should know in advance how much of a discount you are prepared to offer. Do not make this into an opportunity for additional conflict and misunderstanding.

Time Management

Time management can present a major challenge to people leaving academic life for the private sector. This is especially true for those who decide to freelance. Most academics are used to juggling multiple projects that are decided far in advance and there is plenty of autonomy in terms of how many projects to take on. But private-sector clients are not so accommodating. Project requests can come very suddenly, and almost inevitably, everybody wants everything at the same time. Freelance work is particularly subject to spells of feast or famine, and the researcher is sometimes in the position of either accepting work that will push her past reasonable capacity or saying no to a client that may represent a huge stream of future revenue. Whether the client is internal or external, in most cases you'll accept the work, even when you are absolutely certain to face a massive time crunch.

Although deadlines exist in academia, many of them are somewhat fluid and are subject to negotiation. Almost all academic deadlines, whether fixed or fluid, are completely arbitrary, with little direct relationship to proposed decisions or possible actions. Many academic projects begin and end on schedules decided wholly by the researcher, and in some cases, there is essentially no material difference between completing a project at a particular time or a month later or even years later. In general, academic work places primary value on project content and a relatively low value on project timing.

In the private sector, the three-way trade-off of good, fast and cheap is always in evidence. Even the slowest private-sector schedules are pretty quick by academic standards. Private-sector research is conducted so that its purchasers can pursue actions in relatively short-term time frames—this season's ad campaign, next year's product launch, next week's election. In these environments, research results that are not timely are meaningless. Most clients have zero interest in marginally better research that takes significantly more time. Some private-sector deadlines can be negotiated, but the safest operating rule is to assume that they are immovable and that even a successful negotiation for more time may be costly in terms of long-term client relations.

Private-sector research also places emphasis on image, especially the image of being unrushed and unruffled. Clients want to believe that they are getting your best work and full attention. If you constantly remind them that you have other things to do besides work on their project, or if it appears that you just do not have enough time for them, you'll destroy your competent, confident image. Unless you are forced to renegotiate a deadline, never speak in one client's presence of the demands placed on you by others. Model yourself on the bigamist, having multiple relationships while making each of them feel as if it were your only one.

A few tips may help you handle private-sector time management:

1. Be proactive in communications. The only conversations you have any control of time-wise are the ones you initiate. When you make the call, you choose the time, you pick the topic, and you can put limits on the length. When you wait for people to call you, they dominate your schedule and interrupt your tasks.

2. Take advantage of technology. Electronic communications such as voice-mail and e-mail can let you handle many routine communications on a 24-hour basis. If you have a client who needs to be informed of something but who tends to keep you on the phone longer than you can afford, try leaving faxes, e-mails and voice-mail (pick a time when he's certain to be out of the office).

3. Use the business day for business. When you get pressed for time, do only those things during the business day that have to happen during business hours. Shift other tasks to other hours. You can vary the length of your own personal work day, but you do not have control over the hours kept by your clients, vendors, or other business contacts.

4. Take advantage of dead time. Most business schedules are filled with little pauses—waiting for a plane, a fax, for the group to get organized to leave for lunch. There are also big chunks of time, such as airline flights, evenings or mornings by yourself in a hotel, and weather delays, when many of your business activities cannot easily be performed, but others may be facilitated. Anticipate and use these times. Always have a five minute file filled with short tasks for the little pauses. Always have one big "to do" task ready for the big chunks. Do not get stuck in an airport or hotel with nothing better to do than reading *USA Today* or watching some stupid talk show. You would not do these things at home, would you? Well, if it is not worth doing at home it is not worth doing somewhere else either.

5. Make and keep a schedule. Decide what you are going to do and when you are going to do it. Defend your schedule from others and if necessary from yourself. Allow enough time to get each thing done. Do not be overoptimistic about how quickly you will accomplish each task. Realistic time estimates produce functional schedules. Optimistic time estimates are lies. Lying is a sin. And if you do not think God punishes sins, just wait and see what happens the first time you try to explain to a client how come that overoptimistic schedule is falling apart.

6. Understand and live with your own work style. If you like to do your work in big chunks, arrange to get big blocks of time that you can devote to a single task. If you like to hop from one thing to the other, with lots of variety in each work day, find ways to break your assignments into little pieces. Do not try to force yourself into someone else's idea about how to get work done; just be honest and smart about how *you* get work done.

Money Management

Most academic research is done on a fixed-budget basis, and many academics are experienced in handling budgets of this type. Client side private-sector budgets are often managed along the same lines, and most researchers will not encounter many problems in making the transition. Normally academic budgets account for only the direct costs of research and leave other operating expenses to be accounted to institutional overhead. In these environments, researchers do not concern themselves with the fiscal realities of such things as office machines, facility costs, shipping, utilities, or profit margins. Invisible gnomes in the accounting department take care of all that, only emerging now and then to dispute tiny arithmetic errors in someone's expense report form.

Freelancing, however, requires a different perspective on money management. A beginning freelance business will require start-up capital to pay for the initial costs of marketing and to support the research operation through the point at which steady work enables the business to become self-funding. An ongoing business must maintain either a line of credit or operating capital sufficient to keep the corporate body and soul together during slow periods. And to grow, a business must generate profit for reinvestment. If you also want to get rich, you will need to generate even more profit.

It is not enough to simply price your services so as to have enough money; you must also manage money in such a way as to have enough money at the right time. This is known as cash flow. Whereas an academic grant may make the entire budgeted fund available to the researcher at the beginning of a project, this almost never happens in the private sector. For smaller projects, clients may pay only a portion, or perhaps nothing, up front. On larger projects, there will probably be a down payment, followed by progress payments at key points in the research project. Typically one-third to one-half of the total payment will be withheld until after delivery of the final report.

Unfortunately, research costs do not follow the same pattern as research payments. Many costs, such as recruiting participants, designing and printing surveys, and renting focus group facilities, occur before the actual collection of any data and long before preparation of the final report. Also, many vendors of these services offer discounts for swift payment. Thus it is vital to have sufficient cash on hand, either as a cash reserve or as a line of credit, to cover these costs.

The foundation of good money management rests on the twin pillars of good record keeping and good estimating. Good record keeping allows you to track your actual research expenses and gives you ample warning if things are getting out of line. You do not have to be your own accountant, but you probably do need to be your own bookkeeper. Even a simple ledger that merely notes the date, amount and category of an expense is better than stuffing receipts in an envelope and then trying to make sense of them after the fact.

Good estimating is what enables you to charge enough for your services. It is a sad truth of the private sector that everything costs money, and there are an awful lot of things you need to operate a business. Researchers coming from an academic environment are apt to overlook some of these when estimating costs, then find out too late that they have priced their services too low to both cover costs and give themselves a reasonable wage for their time and effort. Some clients actively seek out naive academics for certain projects, knowing that they can negotiate below-fair-market prices. Knowledge is your defense. Project estimates must always have a line (often termed "overhead") that will cover the project's share of all costs that are not direct research activities, things such as rent, office supplies, secretarial support, utilities, duplicating, printing, shipping, taxes, and so on.

The benefits of good money management cannot be overstated. You do not need money problems interrupting the flow of research activities, disrupting your concentration, or keeping you awake at night. It is much nicer to spend your time wondering how to invest your profits than wondering whether or not you are going to have any profits to invest.

7. CONCLUSION

I hope this volume has provided you with some insight into the opportunities the private sector holds for social scientists. I am convinced that there are many ethnographers who can contribute both methodological sophistication and valuable perspective to business problems. And there are certainly plenty of clients with intriguing problems and respectable budgets to offer. It would make me very happy to see a greater flow of new anthropology and sociology graduates into private-sector research positions, as well as to see a greater private-sector presence of more senior researchers. I also believe that a larger acquaintance with the business world would benefit anthropology as a discipline. Businesses, for good or ill, are constantly trying to understand and influence the attitudes and behavior of their customers, employees and stockholders. They provide a laboratory in which methods can be refined and theories put to the test. This kind of testing improves our theories, advances our discipline, and keeps us intellectually honest.

The overall business expansion of the last few years has increased opportunities for social scientists. As businesses increase in size, move into new (especially international) markets, and attempt to meet the challenges of a more linguistically and ethnically diverse labor, they face a greater need for the types of information that ethnographic methods can yield. Sociocultural misunderstandings can cost millions of dollars, wreck careers, and foreclose business opportunities for years. Some choice negative examples from my own private-sector employment history include the following:

A luxury car launch is compromised by Japanese engineers' failure to understand that the scentless leather required for the Japanese market would never be acceptable to the aroma-seeking noses of affluent Americans.

Constant executive turnover at the American subsidiary of a foreign-owned manufacturing firm, due to constant clashes of communication styles, leading to misunderstandings and mutual accusations of bad faith.

And my all-time hit parade winner when an oil company employee brought his wife to Papua New Guinea where a local chieftain attempted to buy her and when rudely refused, effected a temporarily successful kidnapping, followed inevitably by the dangerous recapture of the woman, the employee's angry departure from his company (they had not mentioned this sort of thing when they offered him the expatriate position in New Guinea), huge bribes to calm the tribe, and serious groveling to make it right with the local government authorities.

In contrast, when sociocultural insight informs business activities, the intellectual satisfaction, the glow of making things better for other people, the sense of contributing to a team that builds something can be almost overwhelming. My own list of victory stories includes the following:

After years of consumer research and marketing positioning, I actually saw the first car I'd helped develop being driven down the freeway by an actual honest-to-God consumer and yelled, "That's my car, that's my car!" to my companions.

During focus group work at a copper mine where employee morale was low, my warm-up question, "So, what's it like to work here?" was greeted by a chorus of employees yelling "It sucks!" Our research helped isolate the source of the trouble and we worked with the client to develop an action plan to address it. When I visited again some months later, employees were visibly happier and more relaxed, and the mine was hitting its production targets for the first time ever.

When I worked with a public interest group concerned about the lack of calcium consumption among adult Hispanics (especially women, who are more prone to osteoporosis), focus group research revealed that adult Hispanics were unlikely to consume milk as a beverage, but Hispanic women were very open to increasing their use of dairy products in cooking. A campaign was designed around free distribution of Spanish-language recipes for meals with dairy product ingredients, which proved very successful on both awareness and consumption measures.

The recent economic growth has not only increased the need for ethnographic research, it has increased the budgets available to fund it. Recent trends in business literature have also focused on the human side of the business equation, and terms like "intellectual capital" have largely replaced more mechanistic fads like re-engineering. I genuinely believe that both the need for social scientists in business, and the willingness of the business community to accept and value them has never been greater.

For those who wish to learn more, the References and Additional Resources pages of this book should provide a starting point. In addition, the Appendix section contains examples of some of the types of documents mentioned in the text.

My work in the private sector has brought me many rewards, both intellectually and financially. I have been able to work on important social problems, helped design really cool cars, explored the complex cultural interface of ethnic markets, and helped make big companies better and more humane places to work. But the one thing I miss from academic life is frequent contact with similarly trained colleagues and the shared insights that are only available when researchers get together and really tear a problem apart. There is a fraternity of business anthropologists, but its numbers are small and widely scattered. It is my fondest hope that this will not remain true throughout my working life and that I may someday have the pleasure of working with someone whose career was in some small way facilitated by this book.

APPENDIX A

Example of a Request for Proposal (RFP)

June XX, 19XX

Mr. Able Researcher
Super Social Science, Inc.
1234 Maple Avenue
Anywhere, CA 01000

Dear Able:

In 19XX, the HR function of ABC Company undertook a study to assess the delivery of HR services. At that time we consciously focused only on the delivery of our products and not the actual products themselves. As a result of the study, the HR function is in the process of moving to a leveraged services delivery organization. Concurrent with the final phases of the implementation, ABC's Benefit Planning and Design Staff is beginning to analyze our current health and welfare plan in order to determine whether recommendations for changes are appropriate.

We are interested in working with a consultant to develop a process to identify employees' perceptions of our health and welfare benefit plans including areas of satisfaction and dissatisfaction with the current plans, perceived gaps or discrepancies in the plans' design and employee's suggestions for closing the gaps.

Our intent is to investigate all possibilities and not limit ourselves to the benefits ABC currently offers. The focus is only on health and welfare benefits as the qualified plans (retirement and profit sharing/savings plans) have already undergone a review.

Drivers of the Project

When asked during a recent strategy meeting about benefit plan objectives, ABC's senior management stated that ABC should offer employees a choice of broader, more diverse benefits to respond to ABC's increasingly diverse employee population.

Therefore, we are particularly interested in focusing this project on identifying gaps in which our current benefit plans are not maximizing participant satisfaction from a benefit design perspective. We expect this project to capture both feedback from participants about our current plans as well as recommendations to achieve higher levels of participant satisfaction.

Timing and Proposal Requirements

We intend to begin work on this project upon the selection of a consultant in late July and finish with the reporting of the study by the end of 19XX.

If you are interested in assisting us with this project, please develop a proposal addressing how you can help us meet the objectives of this project. Your proposal should not answer the questions of what changes we should make to our benefit plans but should focus rather on how you envision the process getting us to a list of gaps between our current benefits and where our employees think we should be.

Your proposal should list resource requirements including identification of work that has to be performed by ABC, work that needs to be done by your firm, as well as tasks that can be accomplished by either. We are also interested in understanding your proposed fee and how it may vary as work shifts between ABC and your firm. Please limit your response to no more than 10 pages.

We would also like to see examples of work that you have performed which demonstrate your specific experiences in this area and a list of client references with whom you have worked on similar projects.

Please provide five copies of your proposal by June XX, 19XX.

Upon receipt of your proposal, we will evaluate it based on the following criteria:

- Experience and expertise
- Creativity
- Responsiveness to ABC's needs and objectives
- Cost
- Partnership/synergy

We intend to hold meetings with those firms from which we are interested in gathering more information. We are tentatively holding our calendars open for the second week of July.

Sincerely,

Tom Smith
Vice President, Human Resources
ABC Company

APPENDIX B

Example of a Press Release

**Cultural Considerations Loom Large
in Today's Diverse Workplace**

Recent studies by Super Social Science, Inc., have underlined the important role of cultural factors in the workplace. According to SSS spokesperson Dr. Able Researcher, "Today's managers must not only be skilled in such traditional management areas as finance and planning, they must also gain fluency in the various ethnic and national cultures that are represented in their workforces. Employees who have grown up in different cultures may have differing views about work tasks and procedures, their interactions with managers and supervisors, and even the role of work in their lives."

One recent study focused on supervisor/employee relations in a workplace where employees came from a number of countries and spoke a total of four different languages (English, Spanish, Vietnamese, and Laotian). Focus groups and interviews revealed that employees of Latino and Asian origins paid much more attention to workplace rank and hierarchy than did American-born employees. They were more deferent to their supervisors and tended to expect more deference when they became supervisors themselves. As a result of these differing expectations, workplace conflicts had increased, especially among American-born employees reporting to foreign-born supervisors. Recognition of this problem allowed the company to develop a supervisor training program that incorporated cultural issues. As a result of this program, workplace conflicts have declined, and productivity is on the rise. "This case illustrates the bottom-line impact of cultural factors and how forward-thinking companies can improve their business results by being culturally aware," said Researcher.

APPENDIX C

Where to Learn About an Industry

Industry Journals

Essentially every industry has at least one journal that is widely read by industry participants. These journals provide one of the easiest and cheapest ways to educate yourself and many are surprisingly fun to read. Large university libraries generally subscribe to most of the major ones. Quite a number of industry journals are produced by a single publisher—Crain Publishing. Crain publications include such standards as *Advertising Age, Automotive News,* and *Crain Chicago Business.* Their back issues and special issues can be extremely valuable.

Trade shows

Trade shows provide opportunities for members of an industry to advertise goods and services, attend seminars, hand out awards, make useful contacts, and spy on competitors. Many trade shows are open to members of the general public with payment of a reasonable fee. Others require invitation or sponsorship, which can sometimes be arranged through a friendly contact at a client firm or through the show's organizing committee. Trade shows are a great way to learn about an industry and meet potential clients. You may even be able to teach an informational seminar that will serve as an advertisement for your research services.

Associations

Most industries have at least one trade association, and big industries will have several. Associations can be an important source of information (usually provided free or at low cost), and association meetings and functions can be a great place to make industry contacts. Names of trade associations can be found be reading the major industry journals or by browsing through the *Encyclopedia of Associations.*

Industry Hangouts

Any metropolitan area with a concentration of firms in a particular industry will probably have a few industry hangouts—bars or restaurants where industry participants like to congregate. Most of these gatherings are completely informal, but some are semiorganized; for example, when I worked for an auto manufacturer, I would sometimes attend the monthly industry night at a bar in Long Beach, California, where people from the import auto industry would show up (all the Asian auto manufacturers have their U. S. headquarters in Southern California). If you have your eye on a particular client industry, locating a hangout can be a very entertaining way to get information and contacts. And of course, hanging out in bars has a rich and lengthy tradition among anthropologists, so you can consider it a sort of bridging activity between the academic and private sectors.

AMA

The American Marketing Association is the granddaddy of the research-related trade associations. This association has chapters in all large metropolitan areas and sponsors trade shows, seminars, and publications on a variety of marketing and market research topics. If your area has an active chapter, you should consider joining. Many chapters have dinners or lunches with guest speakers, and usually the organizing committees are searching for new and different presenters. Be sure to offer your public speaking services; this is an excellent way to establish yourself as a local and accessible research expert.

Networking

Everybody talks about networking, but most people don't really use it. The secret of networking is talking to people and getting them to talk to others on your behalf. They can only do this if you tell them what they need to tell others—that you exist, what you can do, and why they should hire you. Be sure that all your friends and acquaintances know about your skills and services. Don't be afraid to ask them who they know that might be a potential client or lead to one. And follow up on every lead you get, no matter how improbable—you can never guess which one will be a winner.

Business Books and Journals

An easy way to educate yourself about business matters is to read about them. There are a number of useful texts, especially in the areas of marketing and market research. Most of your business counterparts will have read these books back when they were getting their MBAs. You need to be familiar with the best known ones. In addition, there are always a few business titles on the current best seller list. Most of these don't amount to much, but you should have a general knowledge of the more serious and successful ones. Their theories, which are inevitably simplified in the process of popularization, often make a good starting point for discussions with clients. Don't directly criticize these theories—your client may have *loved* the book. Just start where the popular press leaves off and describe what you do as *enhancing*, *going beyond*, or *adapting* the theory to the client's particular needs.

Naturally, the most significant business periodical is the *Wall Street Journal*. It's a good source of general business trends and current hot issues, and the editorial pages are hilarious. Other notable business publications are *Business Week, Fortune,* and *The Economist.*

Trade Reference Books

Every client industry will have some trade reference books. Most of the important ones will be advertised in the main industry journals. In addition to client industry trade references, there are reference books aimed specifically at the market research industry. An especially useful source is the Blue Book and its international equivalent the Green Book. These books list market research service providers by location and specialty. If you are planning to freelance, you will want to be listed in these books. They will also be the first place you go when you need focus group facilities or other support services, especially if you get a project that will take you someplace you haven't worked before.

Business Schools

Business schools can be a valuable resource. Most will have extensive business libraries where you can easily get access to texts, references, and periodicals. Instructors may be available for informational interviews. Many business school instructors also run consulting practices, and if your services are complementary to theirs, they can be a conduit to possible clients. In some cases, members of the business community begin their hunt for research services by calling their local business school, either because they don't know where else to start or because they believe researchers contacted through the university will be more scientific. You should make every effort to be among the list of people to whom these over-the-transom projects can be referred.

APPENDIX D

Response To An RFP Using Ethnographic Interviewing and Semiotic Analysis: Proposed Process for Analyzing Nontraditional Qualitative Data Such as Stories and Metaphors

Among the many tools we can use to assist companies in improving business results through people are the techniques and perspectives of cultural anthropology. Business organizations and work groups are in many ways analogous to naturally occurring human societies and communities, and the methods used to study and understand these groups can be profitably adapted to business settings. Anthropological analysis is particularly appropriate to settings where the business culture is undergoing change—

68

either the forced change that accompanies a merger, or the planned change that occurs as a result of a new business strategy.

The following are methods for collecting and analyzing cultural qualitative data:

ETHNOGRAPHIC INTERVIEWING

Ethnographic interviewing is a technique that is specifically designed to elicit insider descriptions of social and cognitive structures within a particular culture. This type of interview shares many characteristics with the laddering interviews common in market research, in that the interview proceeds through layers of description. The technique differs, however, in its emphasis on capturing the vocabulary and descriptive dimensions used within the culture, rather than categories preimposed by an interview protocol. Ethnographic interviews can be very powerful in helping determine what really matters to members of a culture.

SEMIOTICS

Semiotics is the study of signs and symbols. Anthropologists use semiotic analysis to examine the relationships between symbolic actions and speech, the users of the symbols, the meanings the symbols have for their users, and the cultural context within which symbolic actions or utterances occur. An understanding of symbols and meaning can be leveraged to aid communications or facilitate desired culture change.

FOCUS GROUPS

Using focus groups is another excellent technique for eliciting inside-the-culture language and categories. The utility of this technique is dependent on the group dynamic that develops when members of a culture respond not only to an interviewer, but to each other's comments and opinions. While the interview environment is more topic-structured than ethnographic interviewing, focus groups can afford the opportunity to capture insider vocabulary and priorities.

NARRATIVE ANALYSIS

The input from focus groups and interviews, as well as naturally occurring narratives such as letters, memos, speeches, and corporate communications, can be examined through narrative analysis. Software that quickly counts specific words or word strings is used to begin a statistically based examination of the importance of the word or word string in terms of both frequency and context of occurrence. This technique can add a numerical perspective to otherwise qualitative analyses. Having a numerical measurement of key elements of the verbal culture simplifies the task of evaluating change over time, as well as providing a statistical basis for judgment of the relative importance of symbolic phrases and ideas.

APPENDIX E

Example of a Response to a Request for Proposal

Market Research

The employee customers of XYZ's benefits programs present a challenging environment for communications campaigns. The company is diverse in terms of geography, business operations, and employee backgrounds. Conducting market research among representative XYZ employee audiences will enable us to bring an audience-specific perspective to the communication campaign, maximizing its impact and motivational power.

We envision a three-stage research approach coordinated with the specific data needs and timing of the communication waves.

STAGE ONE: XYZ CULTURAL OVERVIEW

Objectives

- Acquire an overview of key XYZ employee audiences.
- Identify defining elements of XYZ's corporate culture and vocabulary.
- Get this information quickly enough to help prepare the content of *Actions* newsletter.

Suggested Approach

The quickest and most effective way to gain an overview of XYZ's culture and employee audiences is to tap into the experience and knowledge of XYZ's Human Resources Generalists (HRGs) and key managers. To meet the needed timing, we envision conducting one minifocus group with the HRGs in Los Angeles and contacting other HRGs and key managers via one-on-one telephone interviews. A total of approximately 20 HRGs and managers will be interviewed during this research phase.

Suggested Timing

As soon as feasible; no later than the week of October 30.

STAGE TWO: IN-DEPTH EMPLOYEE PERSPECTIVE

Objectives

- Gain XYZ employee perspective on the savings plan and its role in employees' lives and in the employment relationship.
- Profile key audiences for the communication campaign.
- Identify important differences between audiences.
- Find motivational "hot buttons" to link audiences with key messages.

Suggested Approach

Focus groups with randomly selected employees would be conducted at several of the major XYZ business unit locations. Depending on the size and composition of the employee base, we envision conducting two or three focus groups at each location. In order to gain the perspective of employees in the highly dispersed sales offices, we also suggest conducting one or two telephone focus groups with them. Based on preliminary discussions, a possible list of focus group locations follows:

Los Angeles
Charlotte
Kansas City
New York
Chicago
San Francisco
Field Offices (by telephone)

Suggested Timing

Several weeks are required to recruit employee participants, develop and approve a focus group discussion guide, and arrange logistics. Because of recruiting conflicts, we recommend that the focus group schedule not impinge too closely on the upcoming holiday season. It is also desirable to do the groups soon in order to have timely information to both inform the communication campaign and feed into planning activities for the Benefits Center. This timing can best be met if the focus groups are conducted after Thanksgiving and before Christmas. If this schedule is not feasible, a second window of opportunity would be as early as possible following the New Year holiday.

STAGE THREE: MESSAGE AND MEDIA TEST AND REFINEMENT

Objectives

- Test a limited number of design and message options with employees before finalizing kits for personal identification numbers and new participants.
- Validate employee understanding of, interest in, and receptivity toward each option.
- Disaster check for unintended offensive or confusing messages.
- Gain employee perspective to fine tune messages and the media for maximum effectiveness.

Suggested Approach

We suggest a limited number of short (one hour or less) focus groups with those employee audiences identified in phase two of the research as the most important or problematic.

Suggested Timing

Late March/early April 1996.

Fees

Campaign Element	Fees
Wave #1	
Market Research	
HRG focus group and interviews	$6,000
Wave #2	
Market Research	
Employee focus groups	$28,000
Wave #3:	
Market Research	
Message and media test	$12,000
Total	$46,000

REFERENCES

American Marketing Association (1996-1997). *Greenbook: International directory of marketing research companies and services.* New York: American Marketing Association, New York Chapter.

Andreasen, A. R. (1988). *Cheap but good marketing research.* Homewood, IL: Dow Jones-Irwin.

Berrigan, J., & Finkbeiner, C. (1992). *Segmentation marketing: New methods for capturing business markets.* New York: Harper Business.

Bradley, U. (ed.). (1982). *Applied marketing and social research.* New York: Van Nostrad Reinhold Company.

Bridges, W. (1988). *Surviving corporate transition.* New York: Doubleday.

Hampden-Turner, C., & Trompenaars, A. (1993). *The seven cultures of capitalism.* New York: Doubleday.

Iacobucci, D. (ed.). (1996). *Networks in marketing.* Thousand Oaks, CA: Sage.

Ivancevich, J. M., & Matteson, M. T. (1993). *Organizational behavior and management.* Homewood, IL: Richard D. Irwin.

Johnson, J. C. (1990). *Selecting ethnographic informants.* Newbury Park, CA: Sage.

Kirk, J., & Miller, M. L. (1986). *Reliability and validity in qualitative research.* Beverly Hills, CA: Sage.

Kotler, P. (1976). *Marketing management: Analysis, planning, and control.* Englewood Cliffs, NJ: Prentice Hall.

Kress, G. J., & Snyder, J. (1994). *Forecasts and market analysis techniques: A practical approach.* Westport, CT: Quorum Books.

Luck, D. J., & Rubin, R. S. (1987). *Marketing research.* Englewood Cliffs, NJ: Prentice Hall.

McQuarrie, E. F. (1996). *The marketing research toolbox: A concise guide for beginners.* Thousand Oaks, CA: Sage.

Spradley, J. P. (1979). *The ethnographic interview.* New York: Holt, Rinehart & Winston.

Webb, E. J., Campbell, D. T., Schwartz, R. D., Sechrest, L., & Grove, J. B. (1981). *Unobtrusive measures: Nonreactive research in the social sciences.* Boston: Houghton Mifflin.

ADDITIONAL RESOURCES

Barabba, V. P., & Zaltran, G (1991). *Hearty the voice of this market.* Boston: Harvard Business School Press.

Bellenger, D. N., Bernhardt, K. L., & Goldstucker, J. L. (1976). *Qualitative research in marketing* Chicago: American Marketing Association.

Berg, B. L. (1995). *Qualitative research methods for the social sciences.* Needham Heights, MA: Allyn and Bacon.

Krueger, R. A. (1994). *Focus groups: A practical guide for applied research.* Thousand Oaks, CA: Sage.

Morgan, D. L. (1988). *Focus groups as qualitative research.* Newbury Park, CA: Sage.

Morgan, D. L. (ed.). (1993). *Successful focus groups: Advancing the state of the art.* Newbury Park, CA: Sage.

Stewart, D. W., & Shandasarri, P. N. (1990). *Focus groups: Theory and practice.* Newbury Park, CA: Sage.

Templeton, J. F. (1994). *The focus group: A strategic guide to organizing, conducting, and analyzing the focus group interview.* Chicago: Probus.

ABOUT THE AUTHOR

MARILYN L. MITCHELL works for Hewitt Associates, one of the world's leading human resources consulting firms, as the head of employee-research activities in the Western Region of the United States. A cultural anthropologist, she holds a BA in biological sciences and a BA, MA and PhD in cultural anthropology, all from the University of California, Irvine. She has extensive experience in qualitative and quantitative research design, cultural analysis, survey development and administration, sampling, statistical analysis, and data interpretation.

She has conducted studies in a variety of organizational, public-policy, business-to-business, and consumer-market research settings in the United States. Conversationally fluent in Spanish and Japanese, she has been Hewitt Associates' primary researcher on studies in Latin America and Japan and has conducted multilanguage, global surveys for Hewitt Associates' clients. She also has lectured on research techniques and interpretation in such forums as the Anderson School of Business at UCLA, the Annenberg School of Communication at USC, the International Congress of Ethnological and Anthropological Sciences (Mexico City, 1993), and the Nissan Summer Institute for Instructors of Historically Black Colleges and Universities (UCLA, 1992).

Qualitative Research Methods

Series Editor
JOHN VAN MAANEN
Massachusetts Institute of Technology

Associate Editors:
Peter K. Manning, *Michigan State University*
& Marc L. Miller, *University of Washington*

Other volumes in this series listed on outside back cover